The

LAB

The Dad LAB

50 Awesome Science Projects for Parents and Kids

SERGEI URBAN

A TarcherPerigee Book

tarcherperigee

An imprint of Penguin Random House LLC
penguinrandomhouse.com

TarcherPerigee with tp colophon is a registered trademark of
Penguin Random House LLC.

Most TarcherPerigee books are available at special quantity discounts for bulk
purchase for sales promotions, premiums, fund-raising, and educational needs.
Special books or book excerpts also can be created to fit specific needs. For
details, write: SpecialMarkets@penguinrandomhouse.com.

Library of Congress Cataloging-in-Publication Data

Names: Urban, Sergei, author.
Title: TheDadLab : 50 awesome science projects for
parents and kids / Sergei Urban.
Other titles: The DadLab | Dad Lab
Description: New York : TarcherPerigee, [2019] | Includes index.
Identifiers: LCCN 2018057938| ISBN 9780525542698 (trade pbk.) |
ISBN 9780525542704 (ebook)
Subjects: LCSH: Science—Study and teaching—Activity programs. |
Science—Experiments. | Father and child. | Parent and child.
Classification: LCC Q164 .U73 2019 | DDC 507.8—dc23
LC record available at https://lccn.loc.gov/2018057938
p.   cm.

Printed in the United States of America
10   9   8   7   6   5   4   3   2   1

Book design by Pauline Neuwirth

To my family: my better
half, Tania, for always
being there for me, and my
children, Alex and Max, for
making me the dad I am

Contents

About TheDadLab

I'm Sergei Urban, and I have two sons, Max and Alex. They were born on the same day, two years apart. Perhaps this is why they're so similar—always wanting to play with the same toy!

In our family, we love creative play, experiments, easy-to-make crafts, educational toys and science experiments, and we do plenty of that. However, I'm not a scientist or a teacher; I'm just a parent, just a dad.

I created TheDadLab, my social media persona, to share with as many parents as possible the creative projects my kids and I do at home, to inspire those parents to spend more quality time with their kids, and to develop a thirst for knowledge and understanding in their children's curious little minds. It all just came naturally to me after I became a dad. I never expected my hobby would lead to any big changes in my life. But people from all over the world seemed to love the activities I posted, and now I am very lucky to be able to make TheDadLab my job while I continue to spend lots of time with my precious boys, getting incredible support from my better half, Tania, and my community.

I hope you and your children have a go at the activities in this book, and that doing so builds happy memories together and lets you see the excitement in their eyes when you unveil a new surprise for them to investigate and play with.

Together with my two wonderful sons, I have done all the projects you can find in this book. Even though I don't have daughters, I hope you won't assume this is all boys' stuff. Not only can boys and girls enjoy all these activities equally, but we need budding scientists of all genders, backgrounds, and cultures.

You can find videos of these and other TheDadLab activities online at www.thedadlab.com, as well as on Facebook, Instagram, and YouTube @TheDadLab.

Have fun, and please share any projects you did with your kids using the hashtag #TheDadLab!

Introduction
Art, Science, and Wonder

Let's be honest: parents never have a lot of free time. So I'm always trying to find projects that require only materials we already have at home (while of course ensuring the activities are fun for my children and myself as well). I've done hundreds of projects with my kids, ranging from classic experiments like the Egg Tower Challenge to more unique activities like Floating Pictures. In this book, I've shared the fifty best projects we've done so far that have produced the most impressive outcomes. I've made sure these activities are simple so no one needs any special skills to perform even the most ambitious experiments, but I really hope you encourage your kids—girls or boys, young or old—to get creative and put their own unique twist on them. Keep in mind, though, that all the fun activities contained herein require adult supervision.

Besides introducing children of any age to science and art, the main purpose of this book—and the aim of TheDadLab activities on which it is based—is to suggest ways you and your family can have fun together. I want to give you ideas for how you can spend quality time with your kids—creating memories, bonding, and just exploring the world together.

These projects give you a wonderful opportunity to enjoy time with your children, and a chance to share something curious to talk about. The educational benefits are just a side effect. You're doing fun stuff, but you're also learning, which is the way we like it in our family.

I've broken this book into several categories, because different kinds of activities will suit different moments. Sometimes you might be short on time and need something that can be done quickly. Or maybe you're all in the kitchen together and you want to seize the moment, grabbing stuff you have on hand right there and then (there's an index on page 177 so you can easily see what you need for each activity). Or perhaps your kids want to do something artistic . . . In the book you can find all sorts of activities you can do at home or outside in the garden!

Many parents get discouraged from doing "science-y" activities with their kids because they think they don't know any science themselves. Well, you don't have to. For one thing, the most important part of science is not knowing answers, but asking questions. You can do this together: "I wonder what would happen if we . . . ?" You might not completely understand what is going on in an activity—and if so, don't feel bad. Scientists still don't fully understand some of it themselves, or didn't until very recently. But in any case, it's OK—you're allowed to answer questions with "I don't know" (although you might want to follow that up with "How can we find out?").

I've done some of the explaining for you. And I've also given some suggestions for how the things you'll see and do might be relevant to the world around you. Like science itself, so much of the fun is in opening your eyes and really noticing. And also like science, no one says it can't be fun.

Enjoy the book!

TheDadLab

Kitchen

EGG TOWER CHALLENGE

Can you get the eggs to plunge into the water without breaking?

WHAT YOU'LL NEED

→ A raw egg, or a few of them
→ A glass filled halfway with water
→ A paper plate or piece of stiff cardboard
→ The cardboard tube from a roll of toilet paper

WHAT YOU'LL LEARN

Objects don't move if they don't have to (this is called inertia).

HOW LONG YOU'LL NEED

20 minutes

? Put a piece of paper on a table and place a paper cup upside down on top of it. Pull the paper slowly and notice how you can move the cup along with the paper. Now try pulling the paper sharply. Why do you think you get different results?

HOW TO DO IT

1. Place the paper plate on top of the glass of water, and put the toilet paper tube upright in the center of the plate.

2. Put the egg on top of the toilet paper tube (on its side, so it doesn't get wedged in the tube).

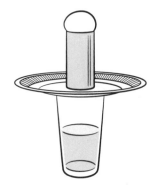

3. Strike the plate sharply from the side with your hand to knock it off the glass.

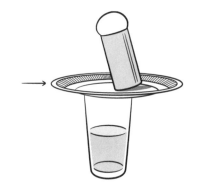

Kitchen ·······

4. The tube will tumble out of the way, but the egg should fall directly downward into the water. If you don't tap the plate away sharply enough, the egg might not fall straight down, so be prepared for some mess (or use a hard-boiled egg, still in its shell).

5. If you're feeling brave, try this with two or three eggs at the same time: Line up two or three glasses of water, set a sheet of cardboard over them, and stand an egg on a toilet paper tube above each glass of water.

 WHAT'S GOING ON?

You think the eggs should be knocked sideways with the plate, right? But all objects have this property called inertia, which means that they resist changing the way they're moving. Think of a heavy weight hanging from a rope—a punching bag or a swing, say. You've got to push hard to get it to move. That "reluctance" is its inertia.

The inertia of the eggs means that, when the plate is pushed sideways and the bottom of the toilet paper tube is dragged with it, the egg at the top wants to stay put—so when the tube topples, the egg doesn't move sideways with it. But now there's nothing holding the egg up! So gravity pulls it down into the water directly below.

MASTERMIND FACTS
Inertia doesn't just mean that when something is standing still, it's not easy to get it moving. It also works the other way around: once something is moving, it's not easy to stop it. That's why when you're on a train, your body keeps moving forward a bit when the train stops, so you have to hold on to the handrail if you don't want to fall over. If a train stops really suddenly, all the stuff on a table in the train car—books, drinks, sandwiches—might fly forward. Oops!

Inertia doesn't, then, mean a resistance to movement. It means a resistance to change in movement. Change is always a bit tough, right?

Why not try . . .

Before beginning a journey, place a shoebox in the back of the car and place a small ball in the center of the shoebox. When the car starts moving, notice how the ball starts moving, too. The ball is actually trying to stay in the same place.

You can also stack a pile of magazines and try to quickly pull one out from the middle without knocking the rest over.

INVISIBLE FIRE
EXTINGUISHER

Snuff out flames with something you can't feel or see.

WHAT YOU'LL NEED

→ Vinegar

→ Baking soda

→ Two tall glasses

→ A row of tea light/
   nightlight candles

WHAT YOU'LL LEARN

A very important lesson:
how carbon dioxide gas
puts out flames, and
when you need to use it!

HOW LONG YOU'LL NEED

15 minutes

HOW TO DO IT

1. Line the candles up in a row and light them.

2. Fill one glass with vinegar to a depth of about
¾ inch.

3. Add a heaping tablespoon of baking soda to the
glass. It will fizz—but hopefully not over the top
of the glass.

4. Tip the glass as if to pour the liquid into the other glass—but don't actually let any of the fizzing liquid pour out. There is something coming out: carbon dioxide, a gas.

5. "Pour" the apparently empty glass over the row of candles and notice how they're snuffed out.

6. If you need more "extinguisher gas" to put out all the candles, you can collect more as long as the vinegar mixture is still fizzing. If it isn't, rinse out the glass and repeat with the same amounts of vinegar and baking soda as before.

⚛ WHAT'S GOING ON?

When mixed together, vinegar and baking soda create a chemical reaction, producing carbon dioxide gas (CO_2)—this is what causes the fizzing. You can't see this gas, but it is being released into the air by the reaction. However, carbon dioxide is denser than air (learn more about density on page 19), so it sinks. When you tilt the fizzing glass over the empty glass, the carbon dioxide flows down into the empty glass, where it will stay, pressed down by the air above. (Over time, the gases will eventually mix—but you're not giving it that much time.)

When you pour the carbon dioxide from the glass over the candles, the gas again flows downward, over the flames. It pushes the air, which consists of oxygen and other gases, out of the way, making a temporary carbon dioxide "blanket." Without oxygen, flames can't burn—and so they go out.

11

MASTERMIND FACTS

Some real fire extinguishers use carbon dioxide for the same reason: the gas coming out of the nozzle blankets the fire and stops it burning. Some other fire extinguishers use dry powder or foam as the "blanket" to stop air reaching the flames, while others just use water—like a firefighter's hose—to douse them.

Carbon dioxide fire extinguishers contain the gas under high pressure. They're good for using on fires caused by electrical equipment—you shouldn't use water or wet foam to put those fires out, because water conducts electricity and could cause an electric shock.

Why not try . . .

Take a bottle and fill it with vinegar to a depth of about ¾ inch. Put 2 heaping teaspoons of baking soda inside a balloon using a funnel. Then, without letting the baking soda spill out, pull the balloon's neck over the neck of the bottle, letting the balloon hang down. Now ask your child to pull up the balloon so the baking soda falls into the vinegar. What happens? Why?

WALKING ON EGGS

Discover how strong eggshells are.

WHAT YOU'LL NEED

→ Several boxes of eggs (ideally two cartons of a dozen eggs each)

WHAT YOU'LL LEARN

Eggs are not as fragile as they seem.

HOW LONG YOU'LL NEED

10 minutes

> Make sure you wash your hands and feet with warm water and soap after this experiment.

HOW TO DO IT

1. Place the eggs in their cartons on the floor, making sure all the eggs are standing upright (with their pointy end up).

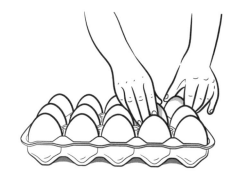

2. Ask your child to stand on top of the eggs with bare feet.

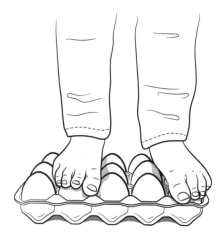

3. If the eggs can hold the weight of a child, can they hold an adult?

4. Will just half as many eggs be able to hold you? If you feel brave, try lifting up one leg while you're standing on the eggs!

 WHAT'S GOING ON?

The phrase "walking on eggshells" tells us how fragile eggs are, and we know it all too well if we drop a raw one on the floor. Yet they can hold up the weight of a fully grown adult without cracking!

The first thing to realize is that your weight is shared among all the eggs you stand on: if your feet are each touching six eggs, then roughly speaking, each egg is carrying only one-twelfth of your weight.

Even so, that's quite a lot! But an egg is shaped to be surprisingly strong if it is squeezed from the right direction. The two ends, especially the pointy one, are more curved than the rest of the egg, and they act like arches, which are very good shapes for sharing weight equally throughout a material so the stress doesn't get concentrated in any one point. That's why arches are used for bridges and for the vaulted ceilings of old churches and cathedrals.

14

It's those stress concentrations that are the problem. When you crack an egg with a knife, all the force is concentrated just where the blade hits the shell, and that will make a crack. But when a weight—like a foot—is placed on the apex of the eggshell, the stress is redistributed evenly throughout the shell.

 MASTERMIND FACTS
Shells are often really tough stuff. Eggshell is relatively weak, because it's only meant as a temporary home for a developing chick, which has to be able to pick its way out once it's ready to hatch. But animals such as snails, crabs, and oysters use their shells as armor to protect against predators, so they make their shells strong and tough.

Oyster shell (mother-of-pearl) is particularly good at resisting cracks because it is rather like plywood; it's made of many sheets of a substance called calcium carbonate. If a crack forms in one of those hard sheets, it doesn't get far before it hits the boundary of another sheet—and there it is easier for the crack to run off sideways, using up its energy splitting the sheets apart. That way, a crack can't easily get through all the layers. We humans copy this layered design to make ultra-tough materials for things like body armor.

Why not try . . .

We think of eggs as being fragile, because they break easily if dropped or struck. But can you break one by squeezing? Ask your child to try this over a sink: have them hold a raw egg in the palm of their hand and squeeze it as hard as they can.

HOMEMADE BUTTER

An experiment you can eat.

WHAT YOU'LL NEED

→ An 8-ounce carton of heavy cream

→ A large jar with screw lid

WHAT YOU'LL LEARN

How to make butter.

HOW LONG YOU'LL NEED

20 minutes

? Did you know that butter's melting temperature is very close to the temperature inside your mouth? That's what produces that tasty, creamy feel when you eat it!

HOW TO DO IT

1. Pour the cream into the jar and seal it tightly.

2. Now have your child start shaking the jar, hard! Give your child a hand and shake the jar yourself if he or she can't do it for long.

3. Eventually, you'll see the cream start to thicken. You can take the top off from time to time to show your child how it's doing.

TheDadLab

4. Finally, it will become so thick that it clumps together in a solid yellowish lump. That's the butter. There will also be a small amount of liquid left (this is buttermilk).

5. Pour buttermilk in a glass, and then the butter can be shaken out of the jar and spread on bread, toast, or crackers. Bon appétit!

 WHAT'S GOING ON?

Shaking the cream in a jar is just the same as the traditional means of butter-making by churning cream in a barrel: turning it round and round with a handle.

Milk and cream are composed of droplets of oily milkfat (which makes up 5 to 10 percent of milk and 15 to 25 percent of cream) floating in water. They don't fully separate, as in salad dressing (see page 156), because there are molecules in the milk that can coat the surface of fat globules to form a kind of membrane, which prevents the globules from clumping together.

But shaking or churning will break up this membrane so, little by little, the fats stick together, making a solid, waxy lump.

MASTERMIND FACTS

The tiny globules of fat floating in milk and cream are what make them appear white. The fats themselves are colorless, but little globules or particles this small will "scatter" the light rays,

17

making them bounce off in all directions. This means that daylight (which is "white light") bounces right back from the milk without being able to penetrate through it, just as it does from white paper.

The scattering of light by tiny droplets—in this case, of water in air—is also what makes clouds and mist look opaque and white, even though the water in the droplets is itself transparent. If the clouds or mist are very sparse, most light rays can pass through, but some are still scattered, creating the visible sunbeams you can see emerging from behind clouds. The same effect makes flashlight beams become visible when they pass through mist or smoke (which is made up of tiny light-scattering particles of soot).

Why not try . . .

Now that you have made your own butter, let's do an experiment on how different materials conduct heat. Take wooden, plastic, and metal spoons and scrape the end of their handles into a block of butter to gather a small blob onto each end. Then rest the butter-smeared ends on the rim of a bowl and fill the bowl with just-boiled water from the kettle. Watch to see which blob starts melting first—that will show you which of the three materials conducts heat the best. Which do you think it will be?

KETCHUP DIVER

It rises and falls at your command!

WHAT YOU'LL NEED

→ A plastic ketchup packet
→ Water
→ A large clear plastic bottle with a lid

WHAT YOU'LL LEARN

How pressure changes the density of air.

HOW LONG YOU'LL NEED

15 minutes

? Can you make an object float just by changing its shape? Try using a piece of kitchen foil or play dough for this experiment.

HOW TO DO IT

1. Squeeze the packet through the neck of the bottle so that it falls inside.

2. Fill the bottle completely with water until it overflows. The ketchup packet floats to the top. If it does not float, you need to find a different packet.

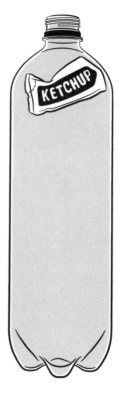

3. Screw on the lid carefully, making sure no air bubble is left in the bottle.

4. When you squeeze the bottle hard, the ketchup sinks to the bottom.

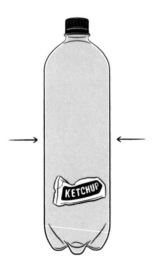

5. Release, and the ketchup rises again.

 WHAT'S GOING ON?

The ketchup itself is denser than water, so the packet would sink if it were completely full of ketchup. But it's not—there's generally a little bubble of air in the packet, too, and this gives the packet buoyancy: the combined density of ketchup plus air plus plastic wrapper is less than that of water, so it floats.

When you squeeze the bottle, the water gets pressurized, but it doesn't really shrink at all: water can't be easily squashed into a smaller volume. But the pressure gets transferred to the packet, too, and the air bubble is much more squishable than the water—it does shrink. So the volume gets smaller, while the mass of the air bubble stays the same. This means its density is increased; now the combined density of the packet is greater than that of the water, so it sinks.

The key, then, is that air (or any gas, generally) is more squishable than water (or liquids in general).

MASTERMIND FACTS

Buoyancy control is crucial for scuba diving. Scuba divers use weights to help them descend through water, because a human body with air in its lungs is actually pretty buoyant. But to get back up again, or to control the rate of descent, divers use buoyancy-control devices, which are balloons attached to the body, generally in the form of a jacket, that can be filled with air from a compressed-air cylinder. The compressed air has a high density, but if some is let out of the cylinder to fill the balloon, it gives the diver more buoyancy. To decrease the buoyancy again, the air can be carefully released through valves.

It's very important to master the art of buoyancy control for safe diving. You need to be able to adjust buoyancy to stay at the depth you want (remember that the water pressure gets higher the deeper you go), and also to ascend and descend at the right speed. If a diver ascends too rapidly, the release of pressure from the surrounding water can make bubbles of dissolved gases form in the blood, which can cause a painful condition called the "bends," as well as breathing problems.

Why not try . . .

Here's another experiment to adjust the buoyancy of an object. Fill a large jar or vase with water and drop in an orange. Does it sink or float?

Now peel the orange (or another one) and drop it in. What happens this time? Why do you think the results are different?

COLOR-CHANGE CABBAGE

Is it red cabbage—or blue?

WHAT YOU'LL NEED

→ A few leaves of red cabbage
→ Vinegar
→ A lemon, cut in half
→ 4 cups water, plus more for diluting
→ Two small glasses or cups
→ Baking soda, in a small bowl with a teaspoon for spooning
→ Powdered laundry detergent, in a small bowl with a teaspoon for spooning
→ A blender
→ A pitcher
→ A sieve
→ Five clear plastic cups or glasses
→ Two droppers
→ Safety glasses

WHAT YOU'LL LEARN

How acids and alkalis can make some substances change color.

> As this is a chemical experiment, it's good practice to have your child wear safety glasses. After all, a stray squirt of lemon juice in the eye would sting!

HOW LONG YOU'LL NEED

40 minutes

HOW TO DO IT

1. Pour the water into a blender. Add the red cabbage leaves. Blend until liquid and strain it through the sieve into a pitcher (discard the solids in the strainer).

2. You should aim to make the liquid not too dark, so the color change is more noticeable, just dilute it with water if necessary. Line up the five glasses and fill them to about 1¼ inches from the top with the strained cabbage liquid.

3. Pour vinegar into one small glass and squeeze the juice of half a lemon into another.

4. Using the droppers, ask your child to squirt the vinegar into one cup of the cabbage liquid and the lemon juice into another. Look what happens!

5. If you'd like, add some more water to the middle glass—this is the "neutral" substance, neither acid nor alkali. Now add a couple of teaspoons of the baking soda to one of the remaining cups of cabbage liquid and a couple of teaspoons of laundry detergent to the final cup.

Again, what happens to the color of the juice?

 WHAT'S GOING ON?
Red cabbage contains a substance called anthocyanin, an indicator that changes color depending on whether it is exposed to an acidic solution or an alkaline one. The more acidic the solution is, the more it goes pinkish-red. The more alkaline, the more greenish-blue. When it is neither acid nor alkali (neutral), it is purple.

? There are a few other plants that can do what red cabbage does in this experiment. Try making a solution with cherries, red onion, strawberries, or turmeric and compare if its color changes the same way.

23

The color changes happen here because lemon juice and vinegar are acidic, and baking soda and powdered laundry detergent are alkaline. The shades may be slightly different because lemon juice is a bit more acidic than vinegar and powdered laundry detergent is a bit more alkaline than baking soda.

You might be more familiar with another indicator: litmus. This dye consists of a mixture of substances found in some lichens. Litmus is often used to stain paper strips, which can be dipped into a liquid to see if it is acidic or alkaline. Like anthocyanin, litmus paper turns pinkish-red in acidic solutions and slightly greenish-blue in alkaline ones. When a solution is neutral, litmus paper is generally a yellowish color.

MASTERMIND FACTS

Color-change indicators are quite common among plant pigments—the stuff that gives flowers and leaves their color. Some flowers that contain these substances can take on different colors depending on whether they grow in acidic (for example, peaty) soil or alkaline (clayey) soil.

Hydrangeas have the opposite color changes to red cabbage: the flowers are typically blue in strongly acidic soils and pink or red in alkaline soil. So you can tell something about the chemistry of your soil just by growing this natural indicator in it.

Why not try . . .

Try testing other liquids in the kitchen to see what color they make when added to red cabbage solution. Just make sure your kids are supervised at all times.

Curious

HOMEMADE MAGNET

How to turn a nail into a magnet using electricity.

WHAT YOU'LL NEED

→ A large iron nail
→ About 16 inches of thin insulated copper wire, with about 2 inches of bare wire exposed at each end
→ C battery
→ A small piece of cardboard (about 4 by 1¼ inches)
→ Sticky tape
→ A pile of paperclips

WHAT YOU'LL LEARN

How electricity can produce magnetism.

HOW LONG YOU'LL NEED

30 minutes

HOW TO DO IT

1. The nail is not magnetic—so it won't pick up paperclips, right? Try it!

2. Wind the wire tightly in a coil around the nail, leaving about 4 inches exposed at each end of the nail. Bend the exposed ends of the wire into a loop.

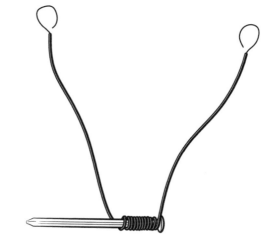

3. Place the battery in the center of the cardboard strip and tape it down. Tape one of the wire loops in contact with the flat (–) end of the battery.

4. Bend up the flap at the "free" (+) end of the battery and press it firmly to make a small dent on the cardboard to see where the center of the battery touches it.

5. Bend the flap back down and tape the other end of the wire to it, but make sure the loop of wire stays uncovered so it will make contact with the battery when the flap is folded up.

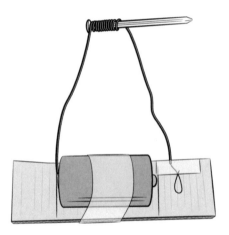

6. Hold the nail just above the paperclips and push down the flap so that the wire makes contact with the end of the battery.

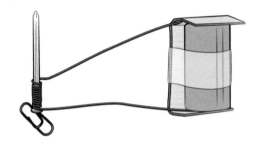

7. What happens to the paperclips now? What happens when you release the flap again, breaking the connection?

? If you take the nail out of your electromagnet, will it still work? To check if the magnetic field is still there, place a compass next to it and see if the arrow reacts when you connect wires to the battery.

Warning: Do not keep the wire connected to the battery for longer than 10 seconds, as it can get very hot.

WHAT'S GOING ON?

What you've made is an electromagnet: a magnet that is switched on and off with electricity.

Electricity and magnetism are closely connected. When electric current flows through a wire, it produces a magnetic field circling around it. This phenomenon was discovered in the early nineteenth century by the Danish scientist Hans Christian Oersted. By coiling the wire tightly, this magnetic field gets more concentrated. And the magnetic field created by the electrical current in the wire makes the iron nail magnetic.

 MASTERMIND FACTS

Electromagnets are used in many aspects of our daily lives, but let's have a look at electromagnetic cranes.

These pick up metal objects using a big, powerful electromagnet: a kind of magnet that can be turned on and off just like in this experiment. That's the way of solving the tricky business of how, once your magnet has collected the metal objects, it can let them go again. Cranes like this are used to move piles of junk metal around at junkyards: with the magnet activated, they pick up the objects (a scrapped car, say) in one place, swing around to where they want to dump them, and turn off the magnet so the metal debris rains down.

Why not try . . .

Try using a longer wire to make more coils on the nail and seeing how it changes the strength of the electromagnet. How does this affect the number of paperclips the magnetized nail can pick up?

29

BALLOON BALANCE

Air does have weight, and here's how to prove it.

WHAT YOU'LL NEED

→ Two identical balloons

→ Three pieces of string, each about 12 inches long

→ A long wooden skewer

→ A pin or toothpick

WHAT YOU'LL LEARN

Air isn't weightless.

HOW LONG YOU'LL NEED

15 minutes

? Try puncturing one balloon near the neck and another in its side. Do you get different results?

HOW TO DO IT

1. Blow up one balloon.

2. Tie a knot in the end. Attach one piece of string to the neck.

3. Do the same with the other balloon, making sure to blow it up to about the same size. Make loops in the string so that you can tie both balloons to the ends of the skewer.

TheDadLab

4. Tie the third piece of string to the center of the skewer and move it until the two balloons balance.

5. Puncture one balloon with the toothpick. Make sure you do that near the neck so that it doesn't pop completely.

6. Hold the balance up as the air comes out (this will make the dangling balloons rotate). Once the balloon has deflated, do they still balance?

Why not try . . .

It's often said that we breathe in oxygen and breathe out carbon dioxide. But the fact is, what we breathe out isn't so dramatically different from what we breathe in: there's about 0.04 percent carbon dioxide in the air around us but about 4 percent in our out-breath. However, carbon dioxide is denser than the air and could influence the results of this experiment. Try using a pump to blow up the balloons with ordinary air and see if it makes a difference.

What happens if you change the temperature of air inside a sealed container like a plastic bottle? Put an empty sealed plastic bottle in the freezer for 5 minutes and see what the temperature change does to it. Or you can place an open plastic bottle in the freezer for 5 minutes, then squash it, seal the cap, and put it in sunlight. As the temperature of air inside the bottle increases, it expands and pushes against the walls. So the pressure, density, and temperature of a gas are all related.

 WHAT'S GOING ON?
We might think of air as being weightless, but it's not. After all, air is not nothing: it is made of molecules of various gases, mostly oxygen and nitrogen. It's true that there are far fewer molecules in air than in the same volume of wood or bread—but they are there, and they do have weight. So when most of the air is let out of one balloon, it weighs less than the other one.

The weight of all the air in the atmosphere is actually really big. On an area the size of a quarter, the total weight of all the air above it adds up to about as much as seven bags of sugar. You have all that pressing down on every square inch of your body!

 MASTERMIND FACTS
Balloons rise when the air inside them is warmer than the air around them. Does that mean hot air weighs less? Not exactly. How much air weighs depends on how much of it you have, just as it does for sugar or water.

What changes as air gets hot is not the weight of the air but its density: how much a particular volume weighs.

Air expands when it warms up. When the burner of a hot-air balloon is turned on to heat the air inside the balloon, it expands so that some of it will leak out of the opening. So there's less air inside it, and the total weight is less. This makes the balloon lighter than the air around it, and it rises. As it cools down again, it contracts, and more air is sucked into the balloon—so it sinks. This is how a balloonist controls how their hot-air balloon rises and sinks.

HOW SOUND TRAVELS

What can you hear underwater?

WHAT YOU'LL NEED

→ A table

→ A musical or squeaky toy (use a mechanical—e.g., wind-up—toy, not an electric one; it's not safe to put electrical devices into water)

→ A bucket of water

WHAT YOU'LL LEARN

How sound can travel through solid stuff.

HOW LONG YOU'LL NEED

20 minutes

HOW TO DO IT

1. Sit at the table. Ask someone to sit across the table from you and gently scratch the table. Can you hear it? Faintly, perhaps?

2. Now press your ear to the table and ask them to repeat the scratching. Is it clearer?

3. If sound can travel through the solid material of the table, how about through water? Put the toy in the bucket and make a sound with it. You might want to seal the toy inside a plastic bag to keep it dry.

? Can you make yourself heard underwater? Try banging spoons together underwater in a bathtub and see if people above the water can hear the sound. What about someone underwater with you— can they hear the sound?

4. Can you hear the toy if it is underwater? How about if you put your ear in the water to listen?

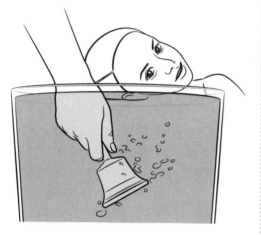

 WHAT'S GOING ON?

Sound usually reaches our ears as sound waves traveling through air. In a sound wave, the pressure of the air is greater at the "peaks" of the wave and lesser in the "troughs." The sound wave is a whole series of these peaks and troughs traveling through air, just like the peaks and troughs of a ripple moving through water. The number of peaks and troughs per second in the vibration is called the frequency. Sounds with a higher pitch (at the top end of a piano scale, say) have a higher frequency.

Why not try . . .

Try making a plastic-cup telephone line? Take two disposable plastic cups, puncture a hole in their bases with a large needle, and thread a long piece of string between them, pushing the string through the hole from the outside. (For a more robust telephone system, use two empty, clean tin cans with holes punched through their bottoms with a nail.) Tie a knot at each end of the string to hold it in place inside the cups. Now have one person take each cup and stand far enough apart for the string to be taut. If one person speaks into their cup while the other holds theirs to their ear, they will hear the voice quite clearly because the sound will pass along the string.

Now let the string go slack and try again. Why doesn't it work when the string is slack?

Curious ·········

In other words, sound is a kind of vibration traveling through the air. But vibrations like this can also travel through other stuff—solids, like wood, and liquids, like water. Because solids are stiffer than air, sound vibrations may actually travel better through them—so you can hear a distant scratching sound better by listening with your ear pressed to the table. (Nosy neighbors sometimes press their ears to the wall to hear the conversations of the people next door . . .) Sound waves can travel through water, too, but high-frequency sounds aren't transmitted so well—the water absorbs them. So underwater sound often isn't very clear.

MASTERMIND FACTS

Whales like to communicate with one another by sending low-frequency sounds through water. The blue whale can make sounds louder than any other animal on the planet, but at a very low frequency, beyond the range that humans can hear. This frequency can travel for great distances through water without being absorbed—blue whales can communicate with one another by sound over distances of several hundred miles. What's more, this communication happens faster than it could for sound traveling through air, because the speed of sound waves in water is more than four times greater than that in air.

But this crucial acoustic communication is getting disrupted these days by ocean "noise," like the sound vibrations created by shipping and other human activities.

ELECTRIC DRAWING

Draw an electrical circuit that will light up a bulb.

WHAT YOU'LL NEED

→ A soft graphite pencil (around 6B grade is right)
→ An 8½ x 11-inch sheet of paper
→ A 9-volt battery
→ 5mm red LED (light-emitting diode; this can be bought in an electrical shop or online)
→ Sticky tape

WHAT YOU'LL LEARN

The graphite in pencil "lead" conducts electricity.

HOW LONG YOU'LL NEED

15 minutes

HOW TO DO IT

1. With the pencil, draw the shape in the illustration—like a Christmas-tree shape, but with a gap at the top. The "trunk" of the tree should be as wide as the two terminals on the battery (about ⅜ inch). Make the lines much thicker.

? Can you think of any other household items that conduct electricity and might be used to connect the battery to the LED?
   Both diamond and graphite are made entirely out of carbon, but what different properties do they have?

2. Draw over the thick lines heavily until they are a strong, shiny black color. Open up the legs of the LED so they will fit over the top of the "tree."

3. Tape the LED in place, making sure the legs are touching the pencil lines. The longer leg of the LED is "+," the shorter one is "–." Label the corresponding lines "+" and "–" at the bottom.

4. Find the corresponding "+" and "–" terminals of the battery. Place the battery on the bottom of the "tree," top down, with the "+" and "–"matching. Make sure the battery pins touch the lines.

5. Does the LED light up? You might see the LED light more clearly if you dim the room light. Now move the battery to the higher "neck" points of the tree. Is it any brighter?

⚛ WHAT'S GOING ON?

The battery can supply an electrical current to the LED to light it up, but only if a conductive material connects them. We're used to metal (usually copper) wires conducting electricity this way, as they do in the cords for our domestic appliances. But here you can see that pencil "lead"—which is actually made of graphite—can conduct electricity, too.

It's not a terribly good conductor, so the LED might not be too bright, but you should see it give out some light. (These LEDs actually only need about 1.8 volts to work, which is less than the 9 volts of the battery, but because graphite is a rather poor conductor, the voltage is much less at the top of the "tree.")

The light will be brighter when the battery is placed higher on the tree. That's because the electrical current has less distance to travel. When it has to pass down a long wire, some of it leaks away.

⚙ MASTERMIND FACTS

Graphite and diamond are made up solely of carbon atoms—but graphite conducts electricity whereas diamond doesn't (it is an electrical insulator). How can the same substance—carbon—conduct electricity in the one case but not in the other?

The answer comes from how the atoms in these forms of carbon are arranged. They are joined up in flat sheets in graphite, and the electrons—the little charged particles that make an electric current—can roam freely across the sheets. But in diamond, the atoms are stacked into a three-dimensional trellis, a bit like a tiny jungle gym. In this arrangement, electrons can't "climb" through the trellis, and they stay stuck to their atoms.

Why not try . . .

Try drawing your own picture for this activity. What could the LED then be used as? Maybe as a monster's eye or a car headlight?

FACE THAT FOLLOWS

They won't believe their eyes when they see this picture of themselves.

WHAT YOU'LL NEED

→ A camera to take a portrait photo
→ A printer to print the image at around 8½ by 11 inches
→ Scissors
→ Sticky tape
→ A mount for the "face"— for example, a dark sheet of construction paper glued onto cardboard
→ A small piece of double-sided tape for mounting

WHAT YOU'LL LEARN

How to trick your brain with an optical illusion.

HOW LONG YOU'LL NEED

20 minutes

HOW TO DO IT

1. Take a portrait photo. The face should be as "face on" as possible. Print it at approximately life size. Cut around the face carefully, making it an ellipse shape.

2. Cut four diagonal slits as shown.

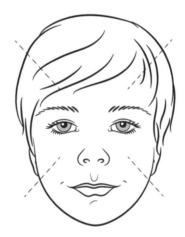

? Half fill a glass of water, put a pencil in it, and look at it from the side. Does the pencil look broken?

3. Bend the photo to stick the edges of the slits together, with tape on the rear side, so that they slightly overlap, making a bowl shape.

4. Trim the overlapping edges.

5. Attach the piece of double-sided tape to your mounting board.

6. Stick on the face. As you look at the face from different angles, what does it look like? The head seems three-dimensional, as though it is bulging outward, not dipping inward.

 WHAT'S GOING ON?

This illusion shows us how our mind is sometimes convinced that it "knows best," despite what our eyes are telling us.

There are visual clues, in the shape of the face and perhaps the shadows, that reveal the face to be concave, like a bowl. But, of course, in everyday life we always see faces that are convex—bulging outward, not curving inward, so our mind interprets the image to make it look like it's popping out.

41

Another famous "face illusion" is the way the eyes in some portrait paintings seem to follow us as we walk around it. Some paintings are especially renowned for this, such as *The Laughing Cavalier*, painted by the Dutch artist Frans Hals in the seventeenth century.

It's sometimes suggested that painters like Hals had a clever trick for achieving this effect. But they didn't really—it can happen with any portrait that looks straight out of the frame. The effect is strongest when the face is shown in strong light and shadow. When we move around an actual person, the shadows look different from different angles. It's a subtle change but enough for our brains to figure out that our position relative to the face has changed—and so has our position relative to the person's gaze (unless they actually move their eyes to follow us!). But the shadows on a painting can't shift, because they are not real— they are fixed in paint. So our brain resolves that in that case, we're always staying in the same orientation relative to the face, with its gaze staying on us.

Why not try . . .

When you get heavy snow in your neighborhood, if you (or your child!) can bear a brief moment of cold, press your face carefully into the snow and slowly withdraw it to make a more accurately molded "hollow face." Is the illusion stronger with the snow face than the cut-out face?

BALLOON LIGHT SWITCH

All you need to light a bulb is a balloon and your hair.

WHAT YOU'LL NEED

→ A balloon

→ A child! (You need their hair . . .)

→ A fluorescent lightbulb

WHAT YOU'LL LEARN

How to make your own electricity to light a lightbulb.

HOW LONG YOU'LL NEED

5 minutes

? Have you ever felt a spark when you've touched something metal after walking on carpet? Why did that happen?

HOW TO DO IT

1. Blow up the balloon.

2. Rub it for about 30 seconds on the child's hair. At the end you'll see that the hair sticks lightly to the balloon.

Curious · · · · · · · ·

3. Bring it very close to the bulb.

4. You should see the bulb briefly flicker with light. (This is clearest in a darkened room.)

 WHAT'S GOING ON?

When you rub a balloon against hair (a wool sweater will work, too), you give it a charge of static electricity. The movement knocks little electrically charged particles called electrons out of the fibers, which can gather on the balloon and give it a charge.

The fluorescent bulb works by an electric current flowing in the gas that is trapped inside the tube. That current is produced by the movement of charged particles, called ions, in the gas. When the bulb is screwed into a light socket and turned on, the ions are pulled through the rest of the gas. Some of them will collide with other atoms in the gas, giving them extra energy, which they then shed again in the form of light. We can't actually see that light because it is in the ultraviolet part of the spectrum. But it is absorbed by a material coating the inside walls of the tube, called a phosphor, which converts the ultraviolet light to visible light.

The charge on the balloon, when it is brought up close to the tube, triggers this same process. Ions inside the tube are attracted to it, and their motion produces the collisions in the gas that generate light. But it only lasts for a flash, because the balloon quickly picks up particles with an opposite charge so that its static electrical charge is neutralized.

 MASTERMIND FACTS
It has been known since ancient times that some objects, such as amber (called *elektron* in ancient Greek), can attract small grains when they are rubbed. This static electricity was used by scientists when they first started studying electricity at the end of the eighteenth century, shortly before the electric battery was invented to supply a more constant source of electrical current. Scientists invented devices for building up a big charge of static electricity, called electrostatic generators, typically using a hand-turned wheel or globe that brushed against a piece of metal.

Rubbing to produce electrostatic charge can create huge amounts of electricity. In fact, electrostatic charging by friction in colliding cloud droplets is what causes thunderstorms: the clouds can build up a massive amount of electrical charge, which is then discharged as a lightning bolt between the cloud and the ground.

Why not try . . .

You can charge other things with static electricity: a comb, for example. Try bringing the charged object close to a small stream of water coming from a tap, without touching the water, and see what happens.

You can put scraps of paper or grains of pepper on a table or a plate and bring a charged balloon close to them to see how they respond.

WHY DO WE NEED TWO EYES?

When you close one eye, is there anything you don't see?

WHAT YOU'LL NEED

→ A lollipop stick, ideally a wide one
→ A blob of sticky blue mounting putty
→ A metal nut, wide enough to get a pencil comfortably through the central hole
→ A pencil

WHAT YOU'LL LEARN

How having two eyes gives us a perception of distance and depth.

HOW LONG YOU'LL NEED

10 minutes

HOW TO DO IT

1. Stick the nut onto the end of the lollipop stick with the mounting putty.

2. Ask the child to hold the stick in one hand and the pencil in the other, with their arms fully extended.

3. Tell him or her to try threading the pencil into the hole in the nut, first with one eye closed, then with both eyes open. Which is easier?

? Did you know that, although they have eight eyes, some spiders have very poor vision? To find their prey, they rely mostly on smell, touch, taste, and sensing vibrations. Some spiders use their webs as a kind of vibration sensor: they can tell where the prey is trapped by the way the threads vibrate.

WHAT'S GOING ON?

We can sense how far away objects are because we have two eyes—giving us what is called binocular vision. Each eye sees a scene from a slightly different angle—you can see this by closing one eye, then opening it and closing the other: look at how what you see changes slightly, particularly where one object in your field of view is in front of another.

Our brains blend these two different views together so that we seem to see just one scene. But as the brain blends these images, it uses the differences in the views from each eye to figure out how far away things are—to give us a sense of depth. If an object is very close to our eyes, what it blocks out is quite different for each eye. Try this with a finger held in front of your eyes, opening and closing each eye in turn. If the object is farther away, there's less difference in what each eye sees—so the brain can tell that the object is farther from us.

If we only see through one eye, closing the other, we lose this depth perception and can no longer estimate how near or far things are. In that case, threading the pencil through the nut becomes harder, because we can't tell if the pencil is in line with, just in front of, or just behind the nut.

MASTERMIND FACTS

The difference in the apparent position of an object when we see it from different angles—as from one eye or the other—is called parallax. This "shift" has long been used by astronomers to figure out how far away stars are. If we look at a star through a telescope at different times of year, when Earth is at different points along its orbit around the sun, the star may seem to shift relative to the more

47

Curious

distant stars behind it. The parallax, like the different views of your finger, is bigger if the star is closer to us. By measuring the parallax very carefully, astronomers can get a pretty good estimate of how far away the star is.

Because other stars are so far away from our solar system, their parallax is generally very small indeed. It's so small that for centuries astronomers couldn't detect it at all, and some of them argued that this meant Earth wasn't moving around the sun (as Copernicus proposed in the sixteenth century), because there didn't seem to be any parallax. They didn't realize just how far away the stars really are, and therefore how small a parallax they will have. It wasn't until 1838 that the first parallax of a star was measured. Today, space telescopes make accurate parallax measurements for thousands of stars to figure out how distant they are.

Why not try . . .

Sometimes our brains struggle to combine the images in both eyes successfully. Here's an easy way to see that. Hold your hands in front of your face and touch your two pointer fingers together at their tips. Now, while still holding your fingers there, switch your focus to something farther away behind them—say, the wall or a window. You should see a double-ended "finger" like a little cocktail sausage appear between your fingertips.

If you now gently move your fingers apart, the "sausage finger" will float in midair between them.

This optical illusion is created by "rivalry" between each eye, as if each is insisting that what it sees is correct. Your brain can't quite figure out where the fingers truly end, and the best compromise it can come up with is the weird "sausage finger."

EXPLORING DENSITY IN A GLASS

What will float and what will sink in this multicolored liquid tower?

WHAT YOU'LL NEED

→ Liquid honey (not crystallized) or syrup
→ Cooking oil
→ Water and food coloring
→ A tall glass
→ Objects to float: a marble, a grape, a Lego brick, a Ping-Pong ball

WHAT YOU'LL LEARN

Different stuff can have different densities.

HOW LONG YOU'LL NEED

20 minutes

? What is denser and what is less dense than water? Make a list of all the objects and liquids in this experiment, sorted by density.

HOW TO DO IT

1. Fill the glass about a third full with water. Mix in the food coloring (blue gives a good contrast with the other liquids).

2. Squeeze the honey or syrup in a steady stream into the glass—it will go straight to the bottom and form another layer. Make that layer fill another third of the glass.

3. Pour the cooking oil in gently to fill the glass. It will float on top of the water.

4. Drop in the objects one by one: first the marble (which goes right to the bottom) . . .

5. . . . then the grape (which goes to the bottom water layer, where it floats on the honey) . . .

6. . . . the Lego brick (which floats between the water and oil) . . .

7. . . . and the Ping-Pong ball (which stays right on top).

 WHAT'S GOING ON?

Density is simply the weight of a fixed volume of stuff: how heavy a cupful is, say. Water is denser than cooking oil, but honey is even denser than water. So the honey goes to the bottom of the glass, then the water sits on top of that, then the oil floats on the water.

The solid objects you add have different densities, too. The marble is denser than honey, so it sinks right to the bottom. A grape is denser than water but not as dense as honey, so it floats at the boundary between them. A Lego brick floats on water but is denser than oil; the Ping-Pong ball is the least dense of all, so it floats on the oil.

Why not try . . .

Here is another way to change the density of water. Fill two glasses with water but to one of them add 2 heaping tablespoons of salt and stir well. The salt makes the water denser.

Now carefully put a raw, unbroken egg into each glass. It will sink to the bottom of the fresh water, because the egg is denser than the water. But it will float on the salty water, because in that case the water is denser.

MASTERMIND FACTS

This experiment uses materials that have different densities. But it is possible to change the density of materials themselves. Density changes if we change the temperature of most substances, like metal, glass, or oil: as they get warmer, they expand and so get less dense, and the reverse is true, too. Water, though, is unusual. It is densest at 39.2 degrees Fahrenheit, and if you cool it down or heat it from this temperature, it starts to expand, getting less dense. That is why ice cubes float in water.

This means that water that has a temperature of 39.2 degrees sinks down below water that is colder. The water at the bottom of a cold lake is, therefore, a bit warmer than the water at the top. That's why lakes freeze in the winter from the top down, not the bottom up. The water at the top might freeze to form a cap of ice, and this acts like insulation to stop the water below from losing more heat and freezing. So a lake can stay liquid underneath its icy surface—which is great for any creatures, like fish, living in it.

Family

HOMEMADE HARMONICA

Get musical with this easy-to-make instrument.

WHAT YOU'LL NEED

→ Two natural wooden broad Popsicle sticks
→ Five rubber bands
→ Colorful sticky tape or similar, for decoration (avoid using paint as it can get into mouths!)

WHAT YOU'LL LEARN

Vibrations can make sound.

HOW LONG YOU'LL NEED

20 minutes

HOW TO DO IT

1. Wrap a rubber band around one end of one Popsicle stick. Make sure that each turn of the rubber band lies flat next to the others.

2. Loop another rubber band onto the stick, end to end.

3. Wrap another rubber band around the other end. Again, make sure that each loop of the rubber band lies flat.

4. Place the second stick on top of the first.

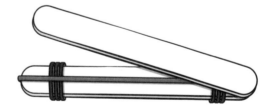

5. Secure the two sticks together with the last two rubber bands, one wrapped at each end.

6. Add colored tape or other decoration.

7. Your harmonica is ready to play! Blow into the gap between the sticks and see what sound it makes.

 What other household items can you use to make music on?

WHAT'S GOING ON?

Sounds in musical instruments are made by something vibrating. This produces vibrations in the air around the instrument, and those vibrations spread out like ripples in a pond. These vibrating sound waves then make your eardrums resonate, which the brain picks up as sound.

What vibrates depends on the instrument. It could be a plucked string on a guitar or a hammered string on a piano. In a harmonica—or a saxophone, clarinet, and other reed instruments—the vibrating part is a flat reed that is set oscillating back and forth by air being blown over it.

In your homemade harmonica, the lengthwise rubber band is acting like the reed. There's a narrow air space between the two sticks propped apart by the rubber bands at each end. Air blown into this gap will set the rubber band vibrating, producing a sound.

It's the same as what happens with a "grass whistle" made by putting a blade of grass between your thumbs and blowing.

56

MASTERMIND FACTS

The pitch of a sound wave—whether it is high or low—depends on how fast the vibration is or how many times it happens each second. The string for the lowest note on the piano vibrates about 16 times a second, whereas that for the highest note vibrates around 8,000 times a second.

This speed of vibration depends on several things. One is how heavy the vibrating object is—the low strings of a piano or guitar are thicker and heavier, the high ones thin. But the vibration rate also depends on how tightly the string is stretched. That's why, if you turn the tuning head for a string on a guitar or violin, the pitch of the string goes up or down, depending on if you've made the string looser or tighter. The amount of stretching in the string is called the tension.

Why not try . . .

Try using a smaller rubber band for the lengthwise one in the harmonica. This will have to be stretched tighter, and so will have more tension. What does that do to the sound?

PAPER ROCKET BLASTOFF!

Journey into space on a puff of air.

WHAT YOU'LL NEED

→ Pads of Post-its, ideally of various colors
→ A pencil
→ A straw with a bend

WHAT YOU'LL LEARN

How to launch simple rockets, but also about propulsion in general.

HOW LONG YOU'LL NEED

15 minutes

? What other things around the house can you propel using only your breath?

HOW TO DO IT

1. Remove a Post-it note from the pad and place the pencil on it, with the sticky side of the paper up and the pencil at the edge farthest from the sticky strip.

2. Roll the note around the pencil to make a tube, with the sticky edge fastening it together.

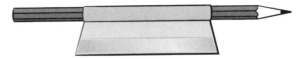

3. Remove it from the pencil and bend one end over.

4. Bend the straw into an L and load the paper rocket on the short end.

5. Blow sharply to launch!

 WHAT'S GOING ON?

The paper rocket is propelled by the gust of air that you blow: it pushes the rocket just like a strong wind pushes and bends a tree.

If both ends of the paper tube were open, the air would rush straight through. But because you closed one end by folding it, the air has something to push against.

MASTERMIND FACTS

Releasing air under pressure is what will send a balloon noisily flying off if you blow it up and let go of the end, making the high-pressure air inside rush out through the neck.

But real rockets are fired into space using a stronger means of propulsion: rocket fuel. There are several types of fuel, but they are generally liquids or solids that burn easily, mixed with substances that help that burning happen by supplying oxygen. All burning needs oxygen, of which there is plenty in ordinary air. When these substances mix and are detonated to start the burning, they produce lots of gas, which streams out of the back of the rocket. Rather like the air streaming from the open neck of a balloon, this pushes the rocket forward. Definitely not one to try at home!

Why not try . . .

Try decorating your rocket by drawing windows or attaching wings or a pointy cone on top.

59

BAG LIFTOFF

Up, up, and away—with your beautiful party balloons.

WHAT YOU'LL NEED

→ Plenty of helium-filled party balloons, perhaps 15 or so
→ A paper gift bag with handles

WHAT YOU'LL LEARN

The principle of buoyancy—and an early understanding of forces.

HOW LONG YOU'LL NEED

20 minutes

HOW TO DO IT

1. The aim here is simple: to tie balloons to the bag until it rises up into the air. If you have a high ceiling, all the better—but don't do it outside, or liftoff will be for good! Perhaps begin by letting your child hold the balloons so that he or she can feel them tugging upward. You could ask, "How many do you think it will take to make the bag fly?"

2. Let the child start adding balloons to the bag, tying them one at a time to the handles. Each time, see if the bag will rise.

3. Need more?

4. We have liftoff!

 WHAT'S GOING ON?

The key question here is why helium balloons (but not air-filled balloons) rise. The simple answer is that helium is less dense than air. But what exactly does that mean?

Here's the important point: a fixed volume of any gas (say, the amount inside a balloon) at the same temperature and pressure contains the same number of molecules as any other gas. Air, helium, carbon dioxide—fill balloons with any of these gases and they will have the same number of molecules inside.

But helium molecules (actually, these are just lone helium atoms) weigh less than molecules of the gases in air (mostly oxygen and nitrogen).

All the same, they still weigh something, so gravity is still pulling them down. But because they weigh less than the same volume of air, gravity pulls on that volume of air with more force than on the helium-filled balloon. This means that, you could say, air will always get "below" the helium balloon, pushing it upward. It's exactly the same thing as what makes some objects, like twigs of wood, float on water: the wood weighs less than the same volume of water, so water will

Family

? If you weigh the bag and weigh yourself, can you work out how many more balloons you'd need to lift yourself off the ground?

Try doing the balloon balance exercise on page 30 with one air-filled balloon and one helium balloon. Is there any way you can get them to balance?

always stay below it. The upward push felt by these lighter-than-air or lighter-than-water objects is called buoyancy (see page 19).

To raise up the bag, the combined buoyancy force pushing all the attached balloons upward has to be bigger than the weight of the bag because of gravity pulling it down. It's just a matter of finding the right balance of forces—just like scales tipping when one side outbalances the other.

Why not try . . .

Let's measure the buoyancy force. If the balloons are all the same size, then the buoyancy force on one balloon is equal to the weight of the bag (weigh it on a kitchen scale) divided by the number of balloons needed to just lift it off the ground. This calculation, as well as offering some simple math, gives an introduction to the central idea of scientific experiments: measuring.

If you figure out the amount of "lift" provided by one balloon, then you can predict how many extra balloons you'd need to attach to the bag to lift it if it had some light object placed inside: you need enough balloons to balance that extra weight. Try it and see if you're right.

That's the other key point about scientific experimentation: it's about making predictions of what will happen, and doing the experiment to check.

MASTERMIND FACTS

Filling balloons with lighter-than-air gases is another way of ballooning, besides heating air to make it less dense, as in a hot-air balloon (see page 32). Helium is a good gas to use, because it doesn't take part in any chemical reactions: it's not poisonous or corrosive or flammable.

In the early days of ballooning, hydrogen gas was also used. But hydrogen is very flammable. So if there was a stray flame or spark near a hydrogen balloon, there was a danger of setting the balloon on fire—which could even happen as an explosion.

This is what happened in 1937 to the *Hindenburg* airship, a gigantic hydrogen-filled balloon used for taking passengers on air cruises. It's thought that a spark from electrical equipment may have set off the fire as the aircraft was docking in the United States. The whole balloon rapidly caught fire, and the airship crashed. Using hydrogen for ballooning stopped very soon after—as did the whole era of airship travel.

GRASS HEDGEHOG

Put it on the windowsill and wait for the spines to sprout.

WHAT YOU'LL NEED

→ A bowl full of sawdust that you can get from a pet shop
→ Elmer's glue or other water-resistant glue
→ An old stocking or pair of tights
→ A small bowl and a large bowl
→ ¼ cup grass seed
→ Two googly eyes and a button for a nose
→ Permanent marker or acrylic paints
→ A plate

WHAT YOU'LL LEARN

How to make a cute hedgehog and take care of plants.

HOW LONG YOU'LL NEED

30 minutes

HOW TO DO IT

1. Cut off a roughly 20-inch length of the stocking leg. Make sure it is open at both ends—cut off the foot section if necessary. Tightly tie a knot in one end. Trim the end of the knot close to the knot.

2. Turn the stocking tube inside out so that the knot is inside. Put the stocking tube in a small bowl and stretch the open end over the small bowl. Pour in the grass seed.

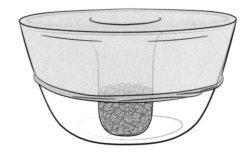

3. Pour the sawdust on top of this. Remove the stocking from the bowl, squeeze the contents, and tie the open end closed. Trim the end of the knot close to the knot.

4. Turn it over so the grass seeds are at the top, and mold to shape so that your hedgehog has a snout. Glue on the eyes using water-resistant glue.

TheDadLab

5. Add the button nose and draw on the whiskers with permanent marker or acrylic paint. Let sit for a while to make sure the glue and paint have dried.

6. Fill the large bowl with water. Immerse the hedgehog to make it damp. Put it on a plate and set it by a window with plenty of light.

7. After a few days, the seeds should begin to sprout through the stocking. Keep watering daily! At some point, the hedgehog might need a haircut . . .

 WHAT'S GOING ON?

This is a fun way to introduce ideas about how plants grow. What do the seeds need in order to sprout? Would it work in a dark cupboard?

You could try making several hedgehogs and giving them different amounts of water and light, to see which grows best.

MASTERMIND FACTS

We're used to the idea that plants need water to grow, but why do they need light, too? That's where they get their energy from. Animals like us get energy from what we eat, but plants use the energy of sunlight. They soak it up in their leaves, where it is absorbed by a molecule called chlorophyll, which gives them their green color.

Plants turn this absorbed solar energy into chemical energy, like

? Do you know what plants need to grow? Name at least three things!

Where do you think is the best place to put the grass hedgehog in your home? Why?

a kind of plant fuel. The plants use that energy to turn carbon dioxide in the air into the materials they're made of, so that they can grow. During that process, which is called photosynthesis, plants produce oxygen gas, which they don't need—so they let it out into the air. That's where most of the oxygen in air comes from.

Plants are at the very start of the food chain. We, and many other creatures, feed off plants, but plants don't have to feed off any other living things: they are the start of life. Without them (and other living things, such as some bacteria and algae, that also use photosynthesis driven by sunlight), there would be no life on Earth.

Why not try . . .

Try molding other creatures. Use acrylic paints or permanent markers to decorate.

HOW TO CATCH A BUBBLE

If you like blowing bubbles and chasing them, you will definitely like this simple trick.

WHAT YOU'LL NEED

→ A splash of liquid dish soap
→ ½ cup water
→ 1 teaspoon glycerin
→ A spoon
→ A cup
→ A drinking straw
→ A pair of socks (or a pair of cotton gloves)

WHAT YOU'LL LEARN

How you can hold bubbles without popping them.

HOW LONG YOU'LL NEED

10 minutes

HOW TO DO IT

1. Pour the water into the cup. Add a good squirt of dish soap.

2. Add the glycerin and stir gently to mix.

? Steel is denser than water, so it should sink. But here is a challenge: try gently placing a small steel paperclip flat on top of the water to make it float. Is it light enough to be held by surface tension?

67

Family ·········

3. You should now be able to dip in the straw and blow bubbles. Ask the child to catch some bubbles on his or her palm and see that they pop.

4. Now give them cotton gloves or socks to put on their hands.

5. What happens now when the child catches a bubble?

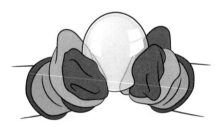

6. You can "play ball" with a bubble, throwing it from one sock to the other, and even squeeze it without it popping.

WHAT'S GOING ON?

To understand why the bubbles don't burst on the socks or gloves, we need first to understand why bubbles usually *do* burst when they touch a surface.

They are a bit like balloons: make a hole in their skin, and they pop! For a bubble, this "skin" is a layer of soap molecules at the surface of the film (see page 69), which is itself mostly made of water. The skin is stretchy—that's why the bubble can be blown bigger. But this skin can't have a free "edge," like, say, a sheet of paper. It has to be attached to something, like a frame you are using to blow bubbles or a surface. Otherwise, the soap film instantly collapses. Try making a loop from a pipe cleaner and dipping it in a bubble solution to create a film of soap in the loop—but instead of blowing a bubble from this, pull both ends of the pipe cleaner loop apart to make a small gap and see if the soap film stretches or pops.

These soap films are fragile and easily broken. But not if the touch is very gentle. The sock's fibers have many tiny hairs poking out—too small to see easily with our eyes, though you can see them more clearly with a magnifying glass. When a bubble settles on the sock, these little hairs will keep it propped up, out of contact with the rest of the fibers—think of a balloon sitting on the bristles of a hairbrush, though much smaller. The hairs will only bend the soap film by a tiny amount at just a few places, and it can withstand those little dimples without rupturing.

 MASTERMIND FACTS

Even the surface of pure water has a kind of skin, where the molecules of water stick to one another. This sticking-together of molecules at the water surface creates what is called surface tension. It's what allows you to slightly overfill a glass, so that the water surface bulges up from the rim without overflowing. The surface tension holds the water in place.

This "water skin" can be supported by tiny hairs, which make the surface dimple without actually puncturing it. Some insects that live by ponds and lakes, such as water striders or water boatmen, take advantage of that to literally walk on water. They are light enough not to sink into the water, but they stay propped above the water's surface—rather than floating on it like a chip of wood—by having legs covered in tiny hairs that don't break the surface tension. Merely floating would be no good to a water strider, because then the surface tension would act like a kind of glue, sticking their legs to the water's surface. As it is, their legs never actually get wet.

Why not try . . .

Another way to hold bubbles is to wet your hands with the soap solution. In this case the water on your hands will also have a layer of soap molecules on it. So when the bubble touches the film of liquid on your hands, those soap molecules can make an unbroken skin with the molecules on the bubble's surface. Then the bubble merges with the film on your hand, and what you get is a bubble dome.

You can even poke a finger, wetted the same way, through a bubble without bursting it, because the soap molecules on your finger help to "keep the seal" in the bubble's skin.

Family ········

PAINTING WITH NATURE

Explore the garden or woods and make art from what you find.

WHAT YOU'LL NEED

→ A piece of cardboard
→ Double-sided tape
→ A dozen or so clothespins
→ Paint and paper

WHAT YOU'LL LEARN

How many different things there are to see and explore in nature.

HOW LONG YOU'LL NEED

2 hours

HOW TO DO IT

1. Cut out a strip of cardboard and stick double-sided tape onto it. When you are outside, remove the backing strip from the tape and go on a nature hunt.

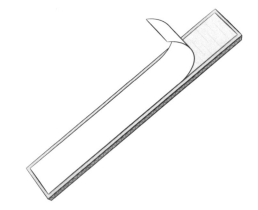

2. Explore the woods and fields, finding anything you fancy: leaves, flowers, pinecones, small stones, twigs, nutshells, feathers . . .

3. Whenever you see something you like, stick it to your sticky strip.

TheDadLab

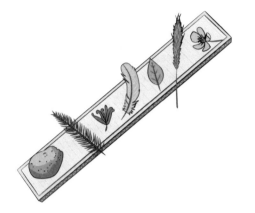

4. Some of these things can then be made into natural paintbrushes by clipping them into a clothespin.

5. Dip it into the paint and see what kinds of shapes and marks it will make on the paper. Some things are good for painting, like feathers. Others might be better for printing with, like pinecones.

? **What is the difference between painting and printing?**

WHAT'S GOING ON?

Talk about what kinds of shapes and textures each object has, and why it is like this. Why should a feather be soft and downy? Why do some plants have broad, flat leaves, while others have thin needles?

The key to this activity, besides simply being outside exploring, is looking: really noticing what is in the natural environment.

MASTERMIND FACTS

Pinecones have particularly interesting shapes. If you look at them from the stem end, you'll see that the scales or prickles are arranged in spirals. Actually, there are two sets of spirals: one turning clockwise, the other counterclockwise. See if you can count how many spirals there are in each direction.

Almost always, you'll find the same sets of two numbers: there might be five and eight spirals in the two directions, or eight and thirteen, or even thirteen and twenty-one in big pinecones. And the amazing thing is that these pairs of numbers are always neighbors in a mathematical series of numbers called the Fibonacci series, which runs like this:

1, 1, 2, 3, 5, 8, 13, 21, 34 . . .

Each number is equal to the two previous ones added together. So it seems that nature knows its math!

Why not try . . .

You can also make brushes from objects you can find at home to try if they paint well. Here are a few ideas: a pipe cleaner, a sponge, pompoms, a folded piece of paper . . .

GETTING INSIDE A BUBBLE

Wrap your children in giant soap bubbles.

WHAT YOU'LL NEED

→ 2 quarts water

→ 2½ cups liquid dish soap

→ 1 tablespoon glycerin

→ A large container for mixing

→ An inflatable baby pool

→ A hula hoop

WHAT YOU'LL LEARN

How to make giant tube-shaped bubbles.

HOW LONG YOU'LL NEED

30 minutes

> The mixture needs to be prepared at least one day before the activity. The activity can be done indoors, or outdoors on a day with no wind.

HOW TO DO IT

1. Mix together the water and dish soap.

2. Add the glycerin. Stir well and leave overnight.

3. Make sure there is no wind outside and blow up the baby pool. Pour in the bubble mixture.

73

Family ⋯⋯

4. Put in the hula hoop and ensure it is well wetted with the mixture.

5. By gently lifting the hoop, you should be able to pull up giant tube-shaped bubbles!

6. They are big enough to place a child inside . . . but it can get messy when the bubbles pop!

 Why are the bubbles in your bath different from the ones that you make using a hoop?

 WHAT'S GOING ON?
Glycerin helps make a particularly good bubble mixture, so that the soap films are strong enough to become big without breaking.

MASTERMIND FACTS
We're used to bubbles being perfectly spherical. But giant ones aren't. How come?

The pressure of the air inside a bubble depends on the bubble's size—or, more precisely, it depends on how tightly curved the bubble is. The smaller the bubble, the tighter the curvature and the higher the pressure.

This means that, for very large bubbles, the pressure inside is really not so different from the pressure outside. It's like a balloon that isn't fully blown-up—it's squishier. So any air movements around the bubble can easily push it out of shape.

Soap films of any sort generally find the shape that has the smallest surface area. That's because it "costs" the film energy to make a surface, and the film finds the shape that has the lowest energy cost. For a soap film stretched between two hoops, like the bubble tunnels we're making here, the surface of smallest area isn't a simple cylinder but one that narrows in the middle: a shape called a catenoid. You might see this shape in the wobbly bubble tunnels you make.

Why not try . . .

You can create giant free-floating bubbles by connecting a couple of pipe cleaners in a large loop, leaving some of the pipe cleaner free to make a handle. Dip the loop into the bubble mixture and then gently pull it through the air. It can take some practice to get the bubbles to detach cleanly.

SWING PAINTING

Make endless swirly pictures with this simple apparatus.

WHAT YOU'LL NEED

- → Water
- → Paints
- → Three poles or canes about 1½ yards long, or a camera tripod
- → Approximately 2 yards of string
- → A few rubber bands
- → A paperclip
- → An empty plastic bottle
- → Scissors
- → A plastic bag
- → Large sheets of paper (11 x 17 or 17 x 22 inches) or a roll of paper

WHAT YOU'LL LEARN

How to make colorful patterns using a pendulum.

HOW LONG YOU'LL NEED

40 minutes

HOW TO DO IT

1. First, make a tripod. Use rubber bands to bind the three poles together at one end. Arrange them on the ground in a stable tripod.

2. Tie a bent paperclip to one end of a long piece of string. This will act as a hook for the paint pourer.

3. Tie the other end of the long piece of string to the center of the tripod.

4. Now make the paint pourer. Cut a plastic bottle in half. Make three holes around the rim of the top half. Thread the string through, secure it with knots, and join the free ends together.

5. Now cut a corner off the plastic bag to make a segment that can be fitted over the mouth of the bottle. Fit it over the bottle and secure it with a rubber band. Cut the very tip off the segment of plastic bag to make a small nozzle.

6. Place the paper on the ground under the tripod and weigh it down along the edges or corners. Attach the bottle's string to the paperclip hanging from the tripod. Make sure the bottle swings clear of the ground.

? Try adjusting the length of the string and see how it changes the drawing. Why would that be?

7. Mix paint with water to make a very runny mixture. While pinching the nozzle closed, pour the paint into the bottle.

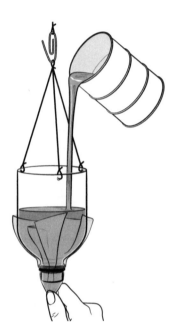

8. Let go of the nozzle and gently swing the bottle so that the runny paint pours out onto the paper below.

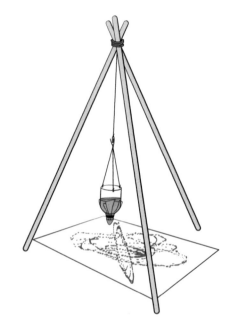

You can add more than one color to the "swing painting."

WHAT'S GOING ON?

The bottle swinging from the tripod is a pendulum, swinging to and fro. But as you and your kids will discover, if you make the swinging weight rotate a little, so that it doesn't just go from side to side like the pendulum in a grandfather clock, the tip traces out interesting oval patterns.

In fact, you'll see from the lines of the paint just how complicated, and also how beautiful, these patterns can be.

MASTERMIND FACTS

Pendulums are one of the simplest pieces of equipment for studying forces in science. Once they start swinging, they keep on going because gravity pulls the weight down to its lowest point, but it doesn't stop there because of its inertia (see page 9).

The time it takes for a pendulum to swing from one side to the other is the same regardless of how heavy the weight is—all that matters (if the swing is not too wide) is the length of the string. The longer the string, the longer it takes for a single swing. This is why pendulums were used in clocks: the to-and-fro swing stays very regular, although it can't continue forever unless given a fresh push.

Why not try . . .

Try painting using sand instead of paint, or just using water to paint on the sidewalk on a hot day. You will need to adjust the size of the hole to make sure you have a constant flow.

PING-PONG LAUNCHER

Fire balls into the air with this catapult-in-a-cup.

WHAT YOU'LL NEED

→ A big balloon
→ A paper cup
→ Scissors
→ A Ping-Pong ball

WHAT YOU'LL LEARN

Elastic materials can
store energy.

HOW LONG YOU'LL NEED

15 minutes

HOW TO DO IT

1. Cut off the bottom of the paper cup.

2. Snip off the top of the balloon.

3. Stretch the hole in the balloon so that it covers
the open bottom of the cup.

4. Tie a knot in the neck of the balloon.

5. Now drop the Ping-Pong ball into the cup. Pull down on the hanging end of the balloon, then let it go to fire the ball upward.

 Another way to get the ball out of the cup is simply to blow into the cup—the ball will jump out. Can you figure out why?

Why not try . . .

Can you fire the ball upward out of the cup so that it falls onto a target, such as into a wastepaper bin or a bucket? You could set up a whole group of target receptacles, awarding points for balls that get fired into different ones.

To show that energy gets transferred into a piece of elastic when it's stretched, take a rubber band—a good fat one is best—and pull on it abruptly to stretch it out until it is taut. Immediately bring the stretchy band to touch your upper lip, just below your nose (take care not to let go!). You should feel that the band has become warm. That's because some of the energy used to stretch it has been turned into heat.

 WHAT'S GOING ON?

What you've made here is really a kind of catapult, with the stretchy balloon "drumskin" acting in place of the elastic bands.

An elastic material is one that will spring back into shape when pulled

Family ········

out of shape and then released. Some of the energy that you use to do the stretching gets stored in the elastic, and when you release it, some of that energy is transferred to the object that you're firing.

 MASTERMIND FACTS

Metal springs will store energy when they are stretched, squashed, or bent, too. That's what happens when you wind up a mechanical watch: the energy stored in the spring is slowly released as the spring goes back to its original shape, and that energy keeps the watch hands moving.

When you jump on a trampoline, energy is stored in the springs (and some in the stretchy fabric) as your feet push the trampoline down, and then this energy is transferred back to your body to fire it upward again.

BANDING TOGETHER

Getting kids to cooperate isn't always easy—but here's a way to help them learn.

WHAT YOU'LL NEED
→ Rubber band
→ Four pipe cleaners
→ Paper cups

WHAT YOU'LL LEARN
How to work as a team. You'll also learn about properties of different materials and the value of friction.

HOW LONG YOU'LL NEED
20 minutes

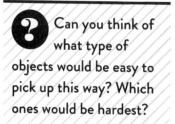 Can you think of what type of objects would be easy to pick up this way? Which ones would be hardest?

HOW TO DO IT

1. Loop and pinch the pipe cleaners in half.

2. Hook each one onto the rubber band at four equally spaced points.

3. Twist the pipe cleaners so that they are securely held onto the band, making a kind of four-legged spider.

4. This is now a tool for picking things up—but only if you use teamwork, with two people each holding two "legs" and pulling them over an upturned cup to grasp it.

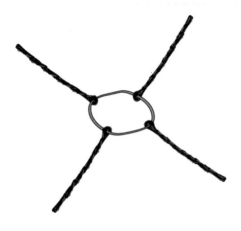

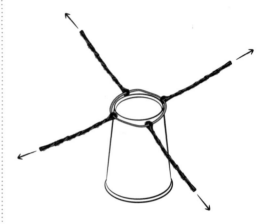

5. You could try stacking cups, and exploring the actions needed to grasp and release objects.

Why not try . . .

Try building a tower using cups and the tool.
Try expanding your team by giving everyone only one pipe cleaner to hold on to.

WHAT'S GOING ON?

This activity is pretty self-explanatory. But there's more going on than you might think. Children have to learn how to coordinate their movements and how hard to pull on the legs to get the rubber band to expand. If they don't move together, it won't work!

You can also talk about how the rubber band is stretchy but the pipe cleaner is not, and about the different materials they are made from. Perhaps ask, "What stops the cup from slipping out of the band, too?" (The answer is friction: a kind of stickiness that stops surfaces from sliding past one another.)

MASTERMIND FACTS

This kind of manipulation task comes pretty naturally to us—even by the age of two or so, we have a sense of how hard to pull and how to maneuver the tool into position. But grasping delicate objects has been a big challenge in robotics.

When we pick up an egg, there's a delicate process of feedback that tells us, via the sensations we feel in our fingertips, when to stop gripping. If we do that too soon, there's not enough friction to stop the egg from slipping out. If we keep squeezing too long, we'll break it. So for a robot hand or gripper to be able to pick up delicate objects without knowing their shape in advance, they, too, have to have some kind of "feedback control" to adjust their grip. Another option now being used in robotics is to make grippers completely from soft rubbery materials that can bend and flex, perhaps using little air balloons to change their shape, so that they've got enough "give" to handle fragile objects.

GUESS THAT SMELL!

WHAT YOU'LL NEED

→ A range of foods you have at home that have a bit of a smell (fruits, bread, chocolate, garlic, etc.)
→ A knife
→ A blindfold

WHAT YOU'LL LEARN

How clever our noses are!

HOW LONG YOU'LL NEED

20 minutes

? Can your nose help you detect danger or things that are bad to eat?

HOW TO DO IT

1. Collect your testing foods.

2. Cut the fruit in half to release the smells.

3. Blindfold your child.

4. Place each item in turn under her or his nose, telling the child to have a good sniff. Can he or she identify what it is?

5. Let them see and eat the items afterward.

 WHAT'S GOING ON?
Smells are produced by airborne molecules coming from the smelly substance and entering our nose. They are sensed by an organ called the olfactory bulb right at the top of our nose, which is actually in the brain, just behind our eyes.

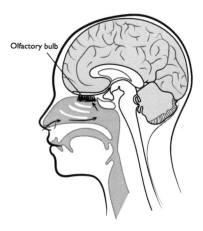

Olfactory bulb

No one knows exactly how the odor molecules are "read" to create a particular smell sensation—but as this experiment shows, we are very good at it!

 MASTERMIND FACTS
The citrus tang of lemons and oranges, coming mostly from the peel, is largely produced by an oily molecule called limonene. It's also used as a

87

dietary supplement, for flavoring in foods, and to give a nice fragrance to some perfumes and personal-care products such as lotions and hand soaps.

The limonene molecule has a mirror-image cousin, different in shape in the same way as a left-handed glove differs from a right-handed one. Everything else about the two molecules is identical. Yet just this tiny difference in shape makes the two molecules smell very different: the "left-handed" limonene smells not of citrus but has a piney odor, like turpentine. How the olfactory bulb is sensitive to these very small differences in the shape or the composition of some odor molecules is still something of a mystery.

Why not try . . .

Our sense of smell is closely related to our sense of taste. To show that, try having your child guess the food by taste only, without being able to smell it. With the child blindfolded, gently hold their nose and then ask them to identify the food from the taste alone. Can they do it?

FOAM BLOWER

Blow a lot of tiny bubbles to make a column of foam.

WHAT YOU'LL NEED

→ A sock (which won't get damaged!)
→ A half-liter-size clear plastic bottle
→ A bowl of water
→ Dish soap
→ A craft knife

WHAT YOU'LL LEARN

How to make a bubble snake.

HOW LONG YOU'LL NEED

15 minutes

? What do you think would happen if we used gas from a helium balloon to blow the foam?

HOW TO DO IT

1. With the knife, cut the bottom off the bottle.

2. Roll the sock over the open end of the bottle and remove the cap.

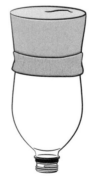

Family

3. Mix a good squirt of dish soap gently into the bowl of water (don't let it get too foamy).

4. Dip the sock end of the bottle into the liquid, then blow through the neck. The bubble snake will emerge from the sock.

WARNING: Make sure your child doesn't suck into the bottle instead of blowing. Keep in mind that children tend to inhale deeply just before blowing and they might suck in the foam by accident.

 WHAT'S GOING ON?

You've made a regular bubble-blower—but with lots of tiny hoops instead of the usual one big one. All the loops of thread in the sock act as hoops that hold a soap film, from which a bubble can be blown. The foam is just a light, fluffy mass of these tiny bubbles joined together.

 MASTERMIND FACTS

Foam is useful stuff, and not just for washing the dishes. Some fire extinguishers use foam to smother fire: the foam settles on the fire and cuts off its access to oxygen, so the fire can't continue to burn.

Foams made from soapy water don't last long before the bubbles burst. But foams can be made from other, more robust materials, too. Bread is a kind of foam. As the dough rises, the yeast in the mixture produces carbon dioxide gas, creating lots of tiny gas bubbles that make the dough expand. When the risen dough is baked, these little pockets blow up into larger bubbles.

Because they have so much empty space, foams can be lightweight. That's why they are used for packaging. Styrofoam is a white polymer, known as polystyrene, that is blown into a foam by being formed within a boiling, bubbling gas. It is usually made into fluffy beads, which can be stuck together to make blocks.

Foams are light and quick and easy to make but also can stay fairly stiff and solid, and some creatures use foam in the wild. The spittle bug or froghopper blows a foam to hide its larvae from predators—this is sometimes seen on plants, and is commonly called cuckoo spit.

Why not try . . .

Blow the longest bubble snake you can. How long is it? If you use a bigger or a smaller bottle, will that make your snake longer?

TRICKY FISHING GAME

Who can catch the most with their fun fishing cap?

WHAT YOU'LL NEED

- → Sticky tape
- → Paperclips, ideally of different colors
- → A small magnet
- → A pipe cleaner
- → A small clothespin
- → A child-sized baseball cap
- → A small bowl or jar

WHAT YOU'LL LEARN

How to make your own game!

HOW LONG YOU'LL NEED

30 minutes

? How many different things around the house can you find that use magnets? What is their purpose?

HOW TO DO IT

1. Fold over one end of the pipe cleaner to make a small loop for holding the magnet.

2. Insert the magnet, twist the pipe cleaner to hold it, and tape it in place to secure it.

3. Sit the child at a table and place the cap on his or her head. Clip the free end of the pipe cleaner to the brim of the cap so that the "magnetic fishing line" dangles in front of them.

4. Scatter the paperclips over the table.

5. The child must "catch" the paperclips with the magnet, moving only his or her head.

6. He or she can put the captured paperclips in the bowl.

7. For a bigger challenge, scatter paperclips of different colors, and tell the child to fish for just one color.

Why not try . . .

Now that you know how to play, you can come up with your own rules of the game. Who is the quickest to collect all the paperclips of his/her color? Who can collect one paperclip of each color? Perhaps if two paperclips of the same color are picked up, you have to start again. Whatever rules you come up with, you're guaranteed some fun family time.

93

WHAT'S GOING ON?

This is a fun magnetic activity that requires good coordination, and the kids will love the business of doing it all by moving and nodding their heads.

Part of the challenge here is that the picking up is being done with the head, not the hands. We're very good at using our hands for tasks like this, but maneuvering our heads is trickier! That's because we have had so much more practice at developing fine motor skills—exquisite muscle control—in our hands, since they're what we use to do delicate tasks in everyday life.

 ## MASTERMIND FACTS

Where do we find magnets in everyday life? You might be surprised at how many are in the house around you. Some clasps for clothes and bags are magnetic. You might have magnetic door fasteners or pin holders. Some magnets are hidden away: they are inside any electric motor (for example, in food mixers and vacuum cleaners) and in computers.

You may well have magnetic clips holding drawings, notes, or other papers to the door of your fridge. But did you know there are magnets inside the fridge door, too? Magnets in the rubbery seal are what hold it firmly closed and well insulated against the warmth of the kitchen.

Messy

STRAW SPRINKLER

The perfect messy experiment for a hot summer's day.

WHAT YOU'LL NEED

→ A glass of water
→ Plastic drinking straw
→ Kebab skewer
→ Sticky tape
→ Scissors

WHAT YOU'LL LEARN

When things are spinning, there's a force that throws them outward.

HOW LONG YOU'LL NEED

15 minutes

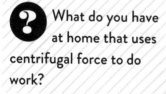 What do you have at home that uses centrifugal force to do work?

HOW TO DO IT

1. Push the skewer through the middle of the straw.

2. Carefully cut a slit in the underneath of the straw about 1¼ inches from the skewer along one side, so that the end section can be bent upward. Make sure to NOT cut all the way through.

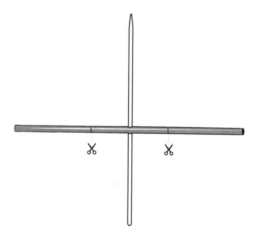

3. Cut the straw the same way on the other side and bend both ends upward.

97

4. Using tape on both sides, fix the two ends to make a triangle. Make sure the ends of the straw are not blocked.

5. Put your sprinkler in the water with the top of the triangle pointing down: the tip of the triangle should be just immersed in the water, but the other two corners still out of it. Then spin the skewer with your fingers and watch the water fly out.

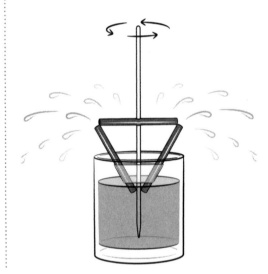

WHAT'S GOING ON?

As you spin the sprinkler, the water that enters through the straw into the lower part of the sprinkler gets pushed up the slope inside the straw until it flies out through the holes you've made at the corners.

What's forcing the water "uphill" here is a force called the centrifugal force. That word *centrifugal* just means "fleeing from the center." It's the same force used in the hammer throw at track-and-field events. The hammer is attached to a wire. The athlete holds the wire and whirls the hammer around and around in a circle—but once the wire is let go, the hammer flies outward, propelled by the centrifugal force.

MASTERMIND FACTS

An object spinning around some central axis will try to "escape" outward because of the centrifugal force—that's what makes an ice-skater's or dancer's skirt fly up and out when they spin.

In big rotating sprinklers for watering crops, the water is thrown far and wide by this force.

Why not try . . .

Spin a small bucket of water attached to a rope; the water will stay in the bucket even when it is tipped sideways—or if it is swung in a vertical circle, so that it is tipped right upside down! The centrifugal force pushing the water outward will stop it from running out of the bucket because of gravity—so long as the spinning is fast enough.

KITCHEN CRATERS

Learn how the moon got its spots.

WHAT YOU'LL NEED

→ About 1 pound of flour (any sort)
→ About ¼ cup cocoa powder
→ Some sprinkles
→ Several pebbles of various sizes
→ A pie pan with a high rim
→ A spoon
→ A sieve

WHAT YOU'LL LEARN

How to make a crater like the ones on the moon (and on Earth!) from cooking ingredients.

HOW LONG YOU'LL NEED

15 minutes

HOW TO DO IT

1. Pour the flour into the pie pan to a depth of about ¾ inch.

2. Make it roughly level with a spoon.

3. Scatter the sprinkles over the surface.

4. Using the sieve, cover the flour and sprinkles with a thin layer of cocoa.

5. From around head height, drop the pebbles one by one into the tray.

6. Remove the pebbles, and you're left with craters among scattered "soil" and "rocks."

7. How do the craters made by pebbles of different sizes compare?

 Can a small meteorite make a big crater? How? What shape would a crater be if a big cube-shaped meteorite hit the moon? Does the shape of the meteorite determine the shape of the crater?

⚛ WHAT'S GOING ON?

It's all intuitively obvious, perhaps—but it's curious, when you think about it, that a powder "splashes" like a liquid. The craters you're making here are a bit like the ones that get formed when a meteorite hits a hard planet like Earth, or the moon.

There's so much energy in those collisions that the rock can actually melt, and it really does splash out like a liquid. Bits of melted and then refrozen rock from very old meteorite impacts on Earth, called tektites, can be found scattered all over the world, thrown for perhaps many hundreds of miles from the site of the impact, like the sprinkles in our experiment. They often look like frozen black teardrops.

101

Messy

MASTERMIND FACTS

Most scientists think that a huge meteorite that struck Earth around 66 million years ago caused such catastrophic changes in the environment and climate that it might have led to the extinction of the dinosaurs. The heat of the impact probably caused huge wildfires, and all the dust thrown into the atmosphere would have blocked out sunlight, stopped a lot of plants from growing, and made the world suddenly much colder. (It's still not clear if this was the only reason, or even the main one, that the dinosaurs went extinct, though.)

This idea was suggested in 1980. Ten years or so later, scientists found what they think was the site of the impact: a crater about 110 miles across, buried under newer rock partly on the coast of the Yucatán peninsula at Chicxulub in Mexico and partly under the seafloor just offshore. It took so long for geologists to find such a huge feature because it was buried. It's thought that the meteorite that created the crater was about 6 miles across.

Why not try . . .

Try dropping pebbles from different heights or throwing them into the pan at different angles.

PAINTING WITH BUBBLES

Create enchanting bright patterns out of foam.

WHAT YOU'LL NEED

→ Food coloring

→ Dish soap

→ Water

→ Plastic drinking straws

→ Large plastic cups (one for each color)

→ White paper

WHAT YOU'LL LEARN

Bubbles and foams have special, beautiful shapes.

HOW LONG YOU'LL NEED

25 minutes

HOW TO DO IT

1. Cover a table to get it ready for paint splatters. Put approximately ⅜ inch of dish soap into each of three cups.

2. Add a small splash of water to each cup.

3. Add a generous squirt of food coloring to each cup. Mix well with the straws.

? What shapes or patterns can you see in your bubble pictures?

4. Place all the cups side by side. Blow into the straws to make a foam that bubbles out from the top.

5. Take straws out and put a sheet of paper onto the foam so that the bubbles touch and color it.

6. Then take it away and look at the patterns. Repeat to cover the whole paper.

7. Another way to make the bubble prints is to tilt the cups and blow into them so that the foam comes out from the top and falls onto a piece of paper beneath.

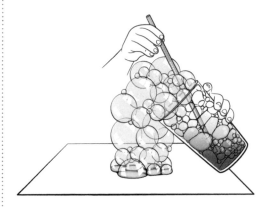

WHAT'S GOING ON?

Bubbles are made of a very thin layer of water. What keeps them from collapsing is the soap.

The soap molecules float at the water surface, all packed together like people standing in a crowd. They make a kind of "skin" on each side of the thin film of water. When the water is colored, the coloring collects in these thin films and leaves an imprint where the bubble walls touch the paper.

MASTERMIND FACTS

Have a close look with your child at the patterns the foam has left behind. Do you notice anything about the way the colored lines left by the bubbles meet and cross?

You'll struggle to find any junctions where four or more bubble walls meet. In general, all the intersections of these lines are threefold, rather like the Mercedes-Benz logo. That's a key feature of foams: bubbles in a layer of foam stick together in threes. If by chance four bubbles come together, they'll instantly rearrange themselves to make groups of three at each junction. That's the shape bubbles "feel most comfortable" with.

Why not try . . .

Try using that bubble picture as the starting point for creating a masterpiece. Use pencils or pens to turn the bubble images into monsters, insects, or houses with many rooms.

Make a greeting card for somebody you care about using these beautiful bubble-painted pictures.

OOBLECK SLIME

Making the weirdest, gloopiest stuff in the world.

WHAT YOU'LL NEED

→ 2 cups cornstarch

→ 1 cup water

→ Large bowl

WHAT YOU'LL LEARN

Some stuff can seem to be both liquid and solid, depending on what you do to it.

HOW LONG YOU'LL NEED

25 minutes

? What do you think would happen if you jumped into a swimming pool full of oobleck? Would you be able to swim?

HOW TO DO IT

1. Place the 2 cups of cornstarch and 1 cup of water together in a big bowl. If you like, you can add food coloring to get colorful oobleck (that's what this slushy mixture is often called).

2. Mix it up by hand. If you still see dry cornstarch, add a bit more water.

3. If you scoop out a handful of oobleck and roll or squeeze it quickly in your hand, it sticks together like putty or clay.

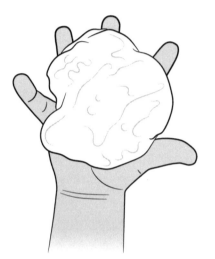

4. But as soon as you just let it rest in your hand, it turns back into liquid and oozes through your fingers.

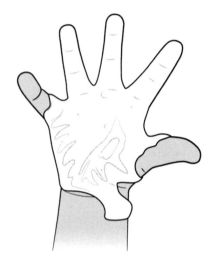

5. Try poking the oobleck in the bowl with a finger: it bounces back, as if the stuff is rubbery, and your finger stays clean. But stick your finger in slowly, and it feels like a runny liquid.

6. Let the kids play and experiment with the oobleck. It'll be messy!

Why not try . . .

Put the oobleck on a tray on top of a big speaker and see what happens when loud sounds are played.

WHAT'S GOING ON?

Oobleck is an example of a "shear-thickening" liquid, which just means that it gets thicker and more viscous when it's stirred. That's because the tiny grains in the mixture—the grains of cornstarch—get locked together when they're squeezed up against one another. If the squeezing happens slowly, they have time to move out of one another's way. But if it's too fast, they just get jammed. It's a bit like trying to push through a crowd: if you try to run through, then you'll probably just collide with other people and bounce back, because they don't have time to get out of your way. But if you walk through, you have time to avoid other people and they have time to move out of your way.

People have been making mixtures like this for a very long time—instant pudding mix, which includes cornstarch for thickening, also makes a (quite tasty) oobleck. But even now scientists are still working out the fine details of how the movements of the particles cause the shear-thickening behavior.

 ## MASTERMIND FACTS

Oobleck is an example of what's called a non-Newtonian fluid. The name comes from Sir Isaac Newton, who studied how normal fluids flow. He found that they keep the same viscosity as they flow, getting neither thicker nor thinner. Water is like this.

But non-Newtonian fluids—ones that are different from those Newton looked at—do change viscosity if, say, stirring them makes them flow. Some get thinner and more viscous as they flow; honey is like this, and so is tomato sauce. But oobleck does the opposite, getting thicker the faster it is made to flow.

Changes like this can be important. Some sandy soils can act like non-Newtonian fluids, which are solid when all the grains just sit packed together but turn liquid-like and runny when vibrated. This can happen when earthquakes shake the ground, causing an effect called liquefaction, where the solid foundations of a building suddenly become anything but—with dangerous results.

TheDadLab

MAGIC CUP

Fill it too far, and it will empty itself.

WHAT YOU'LL NEED

→ Water, colored with food coloring

→ A small piece of blue mounting putty

→ A clear, disposable plastic drinking cup

→ A craft knife

→ A bendable drinking straw

→ Anything to collect water, such as a bottle (unless you are doing this outside)

→ A jug or glass for pouring

WHAT YOU'LL LEARN

How to make water seem to run uphill.

HOW LONG YOU'LL NEED

25 minutes

HOW TO DO IT

1. Using the craft knife, make a hole in the bottom of the plastic cup, just big enough to push the straw through.

2. Bend the straw so it makes a U-shape, then push the other end of the straw through the hole in the cup so the bent end of the straw touches the bottom of the cup.

3. Seal the hole with mounting putty on the outside of the cup—this also holds the straw securely in place.

4. Put the cup on top of the bottle, so that the straw hangs into the bottle.

5. Now pour the colored water into the cup.

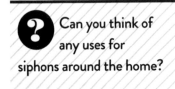

? Can you think of any uses for siphons around the home?

6. The glass holds water, but once it is filled over the top of the bend in the straw, the water will start to run up the straw and down into the bottle below.

7. It'll keep going until the cup is empty (as long as the top end of the straw is touching the bottom of the cup)—the water rises up the straw before falling after the bend.

 WHAT'S GOING ON?
What you've made here is called a siphon. Once the water level in the cup reaches higher than the top of the bent straw, the water inside the straw can flow over the bend and down into the bottle below. And once that flow

has started, it won't stop. Gravity is pulling the column of water inside the straw downward, and as it falls, it "pulls" more water over the bend out of the cup above. This column of water doesn't break, because water molecules stick together. So the water is like a chain being pulled down through the straw.

Meanwhile, this flow is helped along by the air pressure (see page 146) pushing down on the water in the cup. But that's not essential—siphons will also work in lowered air pressure or even in a vacuum.

 MASTERMIND FACTS
A cup that empties itself by siphoning was said to have been invented by the ancient Greek philosopher Pythagoras. The story is that he'd give his students wine—but if one was greedy and tried to take more than the others, he'd be given the "Greedy Cup," which empties itself once it is filled above a certain level.

It's just like the cup you made, with a bent channel like a drinking straw inside, hidden under a tall cap-shaped structure in the center, that simply descends through the stem of the cup to empty underneath it. If you fill the cup too far, the siphoning begins—and all of your drink ends up in a puddle. You can still buy these cups as souvenirs in Greece.

Why not try . . .

Here's another way to get water to run uphill. Place five cups side by side and fill the first, third, and fifth with blue-, yellow-, and red-colored water, respectively. Then connect each filled cup with the empty cup (or cups) that stands next to it using folded-up strips of paper towel, making sure the end dips into the colored water.

What happens after about half an hour? If you already see water in every glass, mark the level of water in each glass and leave them for a few more hours or overnight, then compare how the levels have changed.

FOSSIL DINOSAUR EGGS

Can you free the baby dinosaur from inside its solid shell?

WHAT YOU'LL NEED

→ Toy plastic dinosaurs—
  new ones always work
  best
→ Balloons
→ Hammer
→ Protective glasses

WHAT YOU'LL LEARN

Here's a chance to talk
about dinosaurs, fossils,
and the different ways
baby animals are born.

HOW LONG YOU'LL NEED

45 minutes

*Needs to be prepared a
day in advance,
for freezing.*

HOW TO DO IT

1. Gently pull a balloon over a dinosaur toy,
making sure not to let horns or spikes puncture
it. Choose smaller figures that fit in the balloon
most easily.

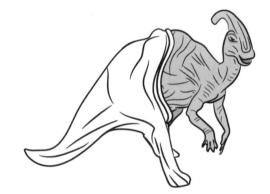

2. Blow up the balloon with the dinosaur inside, then deflate it (this gives the rubber some more flexibility). Pull the neck of the balloon over a tap and fill it with water, letting the water inflate it. Then tie a knot in the end.

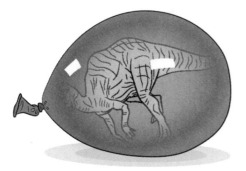

3. It's good to make several eggs at once! Place the balloons in the freezer overnight.

4. When the water is fully frozen, remove the eggs from the freezer and peel off the balloon.

5. Ask the child to wear the protective glasses and let them carefully use a hammer to chip away the ice and release the dinosaur. This is best done outside.

? Dinosaur eggs vary in shapes from spherical to elongated, either with a pointy end like a bird egg or symmetrical at both ends. The smallest dinosaur egg ever discovered was smaller than a chicken egg, while the largest was about 24 inches long.
Can you name other animals that lay large eggs?

113

Messy

WHAT'S GOING ON?

Of course, dinosaurs weren't born from solid eggs. As reptiles, they laid large eggs with a yolk inside, from which their young hatched. But the dinosaur eggs found today are fossilized: turned to stone.

Talk about how some animals (reptiles, birds, insects) lay eggs, and others (mammals) give birth to babies like humans do.

MASTERMIND FACTS

Many fossil dinosaur eggs have been found, some with baby dinosaurs inside. They aren't as big as you might expect—typically around 10 inches long. That's no bigger than the largest known bird egg, made by the ostrich-like elephant birds of Madagascar, which went extinct around one thousand years ago.

In fact, birds lay eggs because they are directly descended from dinosaurs. The dinosaur Archaeopteryx was the earliest birdlike winged dinosaur, which lived around 125 million years ago. It couldn't fly for long distances, only in short bursts. At that time, the skies were ruled by creatures such as pterodactyls and pteranodons. These and other pterosaurs (*ptera* means "winged") weren't really dinosaurs but flying reptiles.

Why not try . . .

Add paint, glitter, flowers, or leaves to the balloons before adding water, to make eggs magical.

Instead of a hammer, you can use warm water to melt the ice.

WATERY WONDER

Pouring water down a string.

WHAT YOU'LL NEED

→ A piece of string, about 18 inches long, that can absorb water (so not plastic)
→ Two clear plastic cups or beakers
→ Food coloring
→ Sticky tape
→ Water

WHAT YOU'LL LEARN

How to pour water sideways.

HOW LONG YOU'LL NEED

15 minutes

HOW TO DO IT

1. First, soak the string in water to get it thoroughly wet.

2. Place one end in each of the two cups.

3. Tape one end of the string just inside the rim of one cup, and do the same to the other end in the other cup.

4. Fill one cup with water and add food coloring. (The color helps to show what is going on.)

> **?** Water can exist in three different states: liquid, solid, and gas. What is water in each of those states called?

5. Lift up one cup so that the string is just (or almost) taut, and then carefully tip it so that the water runs out onto the string. Make sure the string is still soaked and hasn't dried before you start pouring; otherwise, the experiment will not work.

6. The water will run down the string into the other cup.

WHAT'S GOING ON?

The surface tension of the water (see page 166) sticks the water to the string so that it doesn't just run off but flows along the string as gravity pulls it down. Water also sticks to itself (see page 69), which stops it from dripping off too easily.

The way that the water sticks to the string is similar to an effect called wicking, where surface tension pulls water along fibers. But here the water isn't just pulled; it flows down the string because of gravity.

 MASTERMIND FACTS

Just as surface tension can stick water to a string, it can also stick it to a spider's web. In the early morning, water vapor in the moist air can coat the threads of the web with a film of dew, which doesn't fall off because of the "stickiness" between the water and the silk strands.

But the water doesn't coat the whole web evenly. A "tube" of water covering a strand of silk in the web will break up into a series of droplets, spaced out at pretty even intervals along the strand to produce a kind of "string of pearls" effect, especially beautiful as the rays of the rising sun catch it.

Why not try . . .

Here's a way to lower water's surface tension. Fill a bowl with water and sprinkle ground cinnamon onto the surface. Now dip a cotton swab into dish soap and gently touch it to the surface of the water. What happens to the cinnamon?

Quick

MAGIC STRIPS

Paper hoops with a twist will boggle your mind.

WHAT YOU'LL NEED

→ A piece of 8½ x 11-inch paper
→ Sticky tape
→ Scissors

WHAT YOU'LL LEARN

This is a simple first lesson in the mathematical field called topology, which is all about the shapes of things.

HOW LONG YOU'LL NEED

10 minutes

? Can you come up with completely different shapes using play dough that are topologically the same? Keep an eye on the number of holes!

HOW TO DO IT

1. Mark the paper so that your child can cut it into lengthwise strips about 1½ to 2 inches wide. You need three strips for this experiment.

2. Ask your child to stick the ends of the first strip together using sticky tape to form a circle.

3. For the second strip, have your child twist one end before sticking the ends together.

4. For the third, have your child twist the end twice before sticking the ends together.

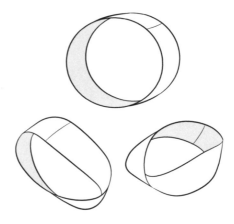

5. Ask your child what he or she thinks will happen if he or she cut all the strips into two down the middle, carefully cutting along the length of each strip. Now ask your child to start cutting to find out. The simple loop is cut into two separate loops.

6. But the single-twist loop, once cut in half, becomes a single larger loop with a twist in it.

7. And the double-twist loop becomes two interlinked, twisted loops.

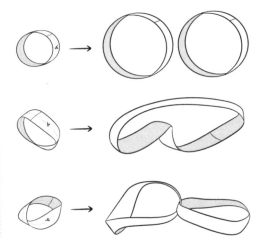

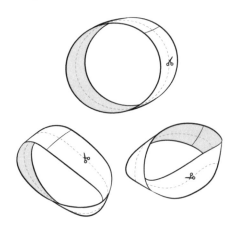

Why not try . . .

To show that the single-twist loop (also called a Möbius strip) has only one side, try asking the child to paint each side of the hoops different colors. That's possible for the simple, untwisted hoop. But as they work their way gradually around the Möbius strip, painting one side, they'll find that they'll just keep going until both sides are the same color and they're back where they started from.

Try also cutting the Möbius strip not down the middle but about a third of the way from the edge. You'll find that you need to cut for two full turns before you come back to where you started. And then what do you end up with?

WHAT'S GOING ON?

The single-twist loop is known as a Möbius strip or band, after a nineteenth-century German mathematician who studied its properties.

The odd thing about the Möbius strip is that it has only one side, and also only one edge. (Prove it to yourself by running your finger around the edge, starting from a position marked with a pencil.) You have to go "around the loop" twice to get back to where you started from—the edge is twice as long as the original strip. By cutting the strip down the middle, you are basically setting this edge free, as well as creating a new one with the cut, so that you end up with a loop that is twice as long.

 MASTERMIND FACTS

Topology is a branch of mathematics that deals with shapes. Two objects are topologically the same if, when they're made of clay, you can mold one into another without making or destroying holes in them. For example, you can change a sphere into a cube that way. But can you make a sphere into a doughnut shape? Only by pressing it flat and pushing a hole through the middle—or by making a hole by rolling it into a cylinder and joining the ends together.

Doughnut shapes are therefore topologically different from spheres and cubes. They're topologically the same as mugs with handles, though: you can mold one into the other just by reshaping the clay without adding any holes.

123

PING-PONG TRAP

Make a Ping-Pong ball follow your commands.

WHAT YOU'LL NEED
→ A Ping-Pong ball
→ Sink with a tall tap/faucet

WHAT YOU'LL LEARN
How the flow of a liquid or gas changes its pressure.

HOW LONG YOU'LL NEED
5 minutes

? What happens if you point a hair dryer upward and turn it on (with the heat set low but the strength on full), and then place a Ping-Pong ball in the stream of air?

HOW TO DO IT

1. Plug the sink and turn on the tap so that it begins to fill with a little water.

2. Place the Ping-Pong ball directly under the stream from the tap.

3. The ball seems trapped underneath the stream of water. It might rotate there but won't escape.

4. If you move the tap, the ball will follow.

Why not try . . .

Tape a Ping-Pong ball onto a length of thread and let it dangle near a flowing tap. If you move the ball so that it touches the water jet, it will get trapped there—you can try to move it away gently, but it will stay "stuck" in the stream with the thread at an angle. You might see that the hanging ball actually seems to be attracted to the water jet—that's because of the way the jet makes the surrounding air move, too, lowering its pressure.

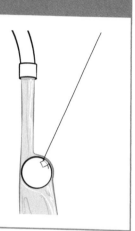

 WHAT'S GOING ON?

This is a demonstration of Bernoulli's principle, named after the Swiss mathematician Daniel Bernoulli who described it in 1738. He figured out that the pressure in a fluid—a gas or liquid—is lower when the fluid is flowing. This means there is a "push" from where fluid flow is slow toward where it is fast.

Here's a way to show this. Take a strip of paper about an inch wide and hold one end just below your mouth. Then start blowing. You should see the strip rise up. This is because the air above the strip flows faster, and so has a lower pressure, than the air below the strip. So the greater air pressure below the strip pushes it up.

In the case of the Ping-Pong ball, the water flowing around the ball is moving faster than the water on which it floats. So there's higher pressure all around the bottom of the ball that pushes in toward the ball's center from all directions and keeps the ball underneath the jet from the tap. What's more, the jet of water drags along the air next to it, lowering the air pressure immediately around the ball. If it moves farther away from the jet, the higher air pressure will push it back.

125

MASTERMIND FACTS

Airplanes use the Bernoulli principle to take off and stay in the air. Their wings have a special shape called an airfoil. If you look at a cross-section of an airplane wing, you'll see that it is flatter on the bottom and more rounded on the top. This means that as the air flows around a moving wing, the flow over the top is more "squashed" than the airflow along the bottom, and it is forced to move faster. Because the air pressure on the top of the wing is less than on the bottom, there's an upward push, called lift. As long as the plane is moving fast enough, this push is strong enough to balance the downward pull of gravity, making the plane stay aloft.

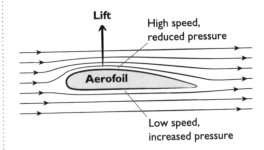

Lift

High speed, reduced pressure

Aerofoil

Low speed, increased pressure

COLOR FROM NOWHERE

Who can figure out how water gets colored just by shaking it?

WHAT YOU'LL NEED

→ Water

→ Food coloring—ideally 4 or 5 different colors

→ Clear glass/plastic jars or bottles with lids, one for each color

→ Cotton swabs

WHAT YOU'LL LEARN

It's a surprise! But how is it done?

HOW LONG YOU'LL NEED

10 minutes

HOW TO DO IT

1. Fill all the jars with water, then put a few drops of food coloring onto the inside of each lid. Use a different color for each bottle.

2. Smear the food coloring a bit with a cotton swab (use a separate swab for each color) so that it doesn't drip off when you put the lid on the jar.

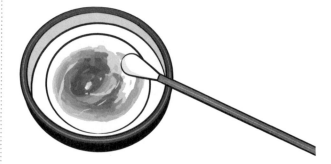

3. Then put the lids on the jars. The jars look like they just have water in them.

4. Now invite your child to shake the jars, and, as if by magic, the water will become colored.

 WHAT'S GOING ON?

Well, it's obvious when you know, right? But see if your child can work it out first. Then he or she can impress their friends with the trick.

 MASTERMIND FACTS

We often learn that there are seven colors in the rainbow—red, orange, yellow, green, blue, indigo, and violet. But in fact, most scientists today recognize just six: the three primaries and the three secondaries. So where did that extra color come in?

Those last two—indigo and violet—are both shades of purple. Indigo is like a deep bluish-purple, whereas violet is a more reddish-purple. But all the colors of the rainbow blend gradually from one to the next: we can't quite say where one ends and the next begins. Indigo and violet are really just blue gradually becoming purple.

? What happens when you mix a primary color with a secondary color that is located just opposite in a color wheel? For example, red and green.

Can you make your own real rainbow by spraying water around on a sunny day?

The reason this bit of the rainbow got split into three and not two is all down to Sir Isaac Newton again, who figured out how rainbows are made from sunlight passing through raindrops. He thought that there should be seven colors in the rainbow, just as there are seven notes in the musical scale.

But why should there be the same number of steps in both of those cases? There wasn't a good reason! Isaac Newton just thought there should be. Now we know better, and most scientists would say there are just six rainbow colors. That's much neater, after all: three primary colors, and three secondary, each made by mixing two primaries. You can see the relationships among all these colors in a color wheel.

Why not try . . .

Once you have the colored waters, your child could try mixing them in a glass to see what colors they make.

LEAK-PROOF BAG

How to puncture a bag of water . . . the dry way!

WHAT YOU'LL NEED

→ A sealable clear plastic bag, e.g., a sandwich bag
→ Jug of water
→ Several round pencils
→ Pencil sharpener

WHAT YOU'LL LEARN

A surprising property of stretchy plastic—and the weird bending of light going through water.

HOW LONG YOU'LL NEED

5 minutes

? If you take all pencils out, water will start pouring out. Do you think that after a while the bag will be completely empty, or will some water still be in there?

HOW TO DO IT

1. First, carefully sharpen the pencils to make them very sharp. Fill the bag with water about three-quarters full and seal it closed.

2. Take a pencil and push it cleanly through the side of the bag into the water inside . . .

3. . . . and out the other side.

4. Do this with other pencils. As long as you leave the pencils in, the holes should stay watertight.

 WHAT'S GOING ON?

The material used to make plastic bags like this is polythene (also called polyethylene), which is the most common plastic used in packaging. Its molecules are long chains of atoms, which are like very tiny rubber bands that can be crumpled up or straightened out. So the plastic is a bit stretchy.

This enables the bag to form a seal around the stem of the pencil. The pressure of the water inside the bag pushes on and stretches the plastic and helps to hold the seal tight.

 MASTERMIND FACTS

You might notice that where the pencil goes into the water, it looks as though it gets sharply kinked. When it emerges on the other side, it seems to kink back in the other direction.

Why not try . . .

Try doing this same trick using different materials. Make the punctures with different-shaped pencils (round, triangular, hexagonal) to see what shape holds the water best. Now use a paper cup instead of the plastic bag and see if the molecules in the paper are as flexible as polythene's—but do it over a roasting pan or the kitchen sink in case the seal doesn't hold!

Of course, the pencil itself stays perfectly straight. It looks bent because light itself bends when it passes from air into water, or vice versa. This is called refraction, and it is why the bottom of a swimming pool looks more shallow than it really is, or why our bodies look weird and distorted when we're partly submerged. Refraction of light by glass (rather than water) is what we use to make lenses for spectacles, binoculars, and telescopes.

SHADOW TRACING

Could you recognize an object from its shadow?

WHAT YOU'LL NEED

→ Paper (8½ x 11 is good)
→ A strong light source: if it's a sunny day, the sun can supply the light, but if not, use a lamp
→ Pencils or pens
→ Objects to make shadows, e.g., small toy animals

WHAT YOU'LL LEARN

How light travels in straight lines.

HOW LONG YOU'LL NEED

20 minutes

HOW TO DO IT

1. This activity is about tracing shadows. Set the toys or other objects on the paper and direct the light so that they cast a shadow on the paper.

2. Draw around the shadow as carefully as you can.

3. If you use a lamp, try moving the object or the lamp so that the shadows have different shapes or sizes. You could draw several shadows for the same object, with the lamp in different places around it.

Quick ·······

4. If you use sunlight to make the shadow, you'll find that it's not so easy to get a big shadow if the sun is right overhead—it works best if the sun is lower in the sky.

 Do glass objects like bottles and tumblers cast shadows? How are shadows different from those of objects that aren't transparent? What happens if you add water to the bottle or glass?

 WHAT'S GOING ON?
Shadows show that light travels through empty space in straight lines. If you imagine straight lines (rays) stretching from the light source—the lamp or the sun—to the paper, the shadow shows where the object blocks out the rays before they can reach the paper. The shadow can look quite different from the object itself—distorted and elongated, say.

You could play a game where someone draws a shadow, or several shadows, with the light source in different places, and then others have to guess what the object is.

MASTERMIND FACTS
Sundials work by measuring the shadow cast by a vertical rod or pointer at different times of day as the sun moves across the sky. The sun comes up in the east, moves higher in the sky toward noon, and then sets in the west. (It's not really the sun that's moving. It looks that way, but actually the apparent motion is caused by Earth's rotation.) As the sun's position in the sky changes, so does the position of the pointer's shadow on the ground—it points to different places at different times of day. So the shadow can act like a kind of hour hand on a clock.

The most common type of sundial, like those you can sometimes see in gardens (especially of stately homes), has a slanted "pointer" (called a gnomon) on a round horizontal plate with the hours marked on it. If you see one of these, you'll notice that the hour markings aren't spaced regularly like those on a clock or watch face.

These sundials are only accurate for the particular latitude they're made for—a sundial made for use in London wouldn't tell the time properly in Egypt.

Why not try . . .

Try tracing the shadow of a person—in sunlight with chalk on the ground at one time of day, and then again for the same person standing in exactly the same spot a few hours later. How are they different?

THE POWER OF MAGNETS

If we put something between a metal object and a magnet, would the magnet still stick?

WHAT YOU'LL NEED

- → A big pile of paperclips (100 or so)
- → A strong magnet or a bunch of small ones together
- → A small book or a magazine

WHAT YOU'LL LEARN

Magnetic force can go through objects.

HOW LONG YOU'LL NEED

10 minutes

HOW TO DO IT

1. Pour the paperclips into a pile.

2. Have your child hold a hand over the pile of paperclips. Are paperclips attracted to a bare, open hand? Of course not!

3. But then have him or her place their hand on top of the pile and put the magnet on the top.

4. As the child raises their hand, the paperclips come, too, dangling in long chains. (Don't worry—the magnetic force won't do any harm as it passes through your child's hand.)

? Try comparing different magnets you might have. Which one is the strongest? You can find out by checking how many paperclips are magnetically sticking to one another.

5. Try it with a book placed on top of the pile and the magnet placed on the book.

6. Watch as your child plucks the magnet off their hand or the book and all the paperclips fall back down. Or let the paperclips cover the magnet itself, and they can be molded almost like clay.

Quick ⋯⋯⋯

WHAT'S GOING ON?

Magnets produce a magnetic force that attracts iron and steel—that's what the paperclips are made from. If the magnet is strong enough, this force can pass right through objects such as a hand or a book.

MASTERMIND FACTS

When a metal object like a paperclip is close to a magnet, it too can be made magnetic, and so other paperclips will be attracted to it.

In fact, you can make a steel needle into a kind of magnet by touching the needle with a strong magnet and gently "stroking" the magnet along the needle repeatedly in the same direction. If you then push the needle through a cork and let it float on water, it will act as a compass, lining up to point toward the North Pole because of the force produced by Earth's own magnetic field. But the needle will gradually lose its magnetism again.

Why not try . . .

Not all metals are magnetic. You could experiment to see which is magnetic and which is not, using different coins, keys, cutlery, metal pipes, and so on.

THE UNSINKABLE SHIP

WHAT YOU'LL NEED

→ A piece of paper about 3 x 4 inches

→ A large glass bowl full of water

→ A glass or a small bowl

WHAT YOU'LL LEARN

How to keep air inside containers underwater.

HOW LONG YOU'LL NEED

10 minutes

? Did you know that the oldest illustration of origami (paper folding) in Europe was made by Johannes de Sacrobosco in 1490, and that it showed a paper boat just like the one you are making in this project?

HOW TO DO IT

1. Follow the instructions to make a paper boat. If you use a 3 x 4-inch paper, the boat should fit into a regular glass.

139

2. Let the boat float on the water in the bowl.

3. Place the inverted glass over it.

4. Keep lowering the glass, with the boat inside, into the water until the rim touches the bottom of the bowl.

5. Then carefully lift the glass back up again.

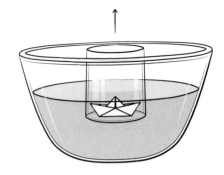

The boat seems to have been pushed right underwater, but when the glass is taken away, it is still dry on top, with no water trapped inside. How come?

WHAT'S GOING ON?

The boat stays in the bubble of air trapped in the glass. When the glass and boat reach the bottom of the bowl, it looks as though they are fully submerged. But in fact, the glass is full of air, not water.

We think of the glass as being "empty" if there's no water in it, but, in fact, it is full of air, and the air can't go anywhere as long as the glass is kept inverted. So the inside stays dry, even though it is beneath the water's surface.

MASTERMIND FACTS

What we've made here is a diving bell. This was the earliest kind of "submarine" for letting people survive underwater. Some old records say that the ancient Greeks used glass diving bells to explore under the Mediterranean Sea, but we don't know for sure. The first modern diving bells, which would be lowered under the water with people inside, were made in the sixteenth century. They have to be carefully weighted to make sure they don't tip over and let the air bubble escape.

But the oxygen in the air, which divers need to survive, gets used up as they breathe, and so they can't stay submerged for very long unless fresh air can be pumped down to them through a tube—or supplied from compressed-air cylinders on the bell. Diving bells are still used today for undersea exploration.

Why not try . . .

Make a diver to take down in a diving bell by drawing a face on a Ping-Pong ball and floating it in the bowl. If you submerge a clear plastic cup inverted over the top of the ball, it stays full of air with the ball at the bottom, as with the ship. But what if you cut a small hole in the top (that is, the bottom!) of the cup? And what if you place your finger to cover the hole before submerging, and then remove it to open the hole?

THE BOUNCING MARBLE

Make a small drum for a marble to play sounds.

WHAT YOU'LL NEED

→ A glass tumbler, ideally with a wide rim
→ A balloon
→ Scissors
→ A rubber band
→ A marble

WHAT YOU'LL LEARN

How to make a simple bouncing toy that looks and sounds great!

HOW LONG YOU'LL NEED

10 minutes

HOW TO DO IT

1. Fold the balloon in half and cut off one corner to make a large hole in it.

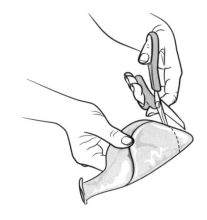

2. Stretch the balloon skin over the tumbler.

3. Secure it with the rubber band.

4. Drop the marble onto the "drumskin" from a height about 6 inches above it.

5. Watch it bounce—and listen to the sound it makes!

> **?** Listen to the "beats of the drum" as the marble bounces. What do you notice about the timing between each beat? Why do you think it changes?

 WHAT'S GOING ON?

You have made a miniature trampoline for marbles! It's also a kind of drum: as the marble strikes the balloon skin, it becomes a beater that makes the rubber skin vibrate like a drumhead.

Every time the marble hits the balloon skin, the skin is pushed downward and stores energy in the stretched rubber, which is then used to fire the marble back upward as if from a catapult. But on each bounce, a small bit of the energy gets lost—mostly as heat, which warms up the balloon skin a little, but also as sound in the sound waves made by the marble's impact on the skin. So on each bounce, the marble rebounds a little less high, until eventually it comes to rest.

If instead of bouncing off the skin, the marble lands near the edge, it bounces back toward the center. That's because, although the skin is flat to begin with, the little dimple that forms as the descending marble strikes near the rim will be slightly asymmetrical. The skin is "held up" on the side nearest the rim, so the marble is catapulted upward at an angle, tilting gently back toward the center.

143

MASTERMIND FACTS

The sound that a drum makes depends on how big it is—a bigger drum will generally make a deeper sound, just as a double bass sounds deeper than a violin. But the sound also depends on how tight the drumskin is: if it is tighter, the sound is higher, just as it is for a guitar string or a plucked rubber band.

Some drums, such as the big kettledrums (timpani) in orchestras or the tabla drums used in traditional Indian music, have to be carefully tuned so the drumskin makes the right note when it is beaten. Tabla drums have wooden pegs that are moved up and down to adjust the tightness of the straps holding the drumskin in place. Modern timpani have a foot pedal that can be pressed to adjust the tuning by pulling on or loosening the hoop holding the drumskin in place.

Why not try . . .

Take a second, identical glass, but this time, instead of covering it with a balloon, cover it completely with crisscrossed strips of tape. Now you have two drums to compare. Which one makes a marble jump more? Do they sound the same?

GRAVITY-DEFYING BOTTLE

Turn the bottle upside down, and the Ping-Pong ball doesn't fall off the top.

WHAT YOU'LL NEED

→ Water
→ A glass bottle, about milk-bottle size, with a neck wide enough to hold a Ping-Pong ball
→ A Ping-Pong ball
→ Large tray with a rim, to catch spillage

WHAT YOU'LL LEARN

The "sucking power" of a vacuum.

HOW LONG YOU'LL NEED

10 minutes

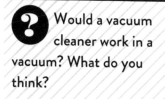 Would a vacuum cleaner work in a vacuum? What do you think?

HOW TO DO IT

1. Stand the bottle in the tray and totally fill the bottle with water until it is almost overflowing.

2. Place the Ping-Pong ball on the neck.

145

3. Then turn the bottle upside down.

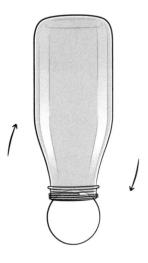

4. The Ping-Pong ball stays there!

5. Remove the ball when the bottle is upside down to see how water is getting out.

⚛ WHAT'S GOING ON?

For water to come out of the bottle, something has to replace it. Normally air will do that, but it can't in this case because the Ping-Pong ball is blocking the neck of the bottle.

Why does something have to replace the water, though? Why can't it just run out anyway, given that gravity is pulling it down? If the water was pulled from the bottle without anything replacing it, this would leave behind a vacuum—a bit of space with nothing, not even air, in it. It takes a lot of force to make that happen, and in this case gravity is not strong enough to do that.

The ancient Greek philosopher Aristotle said that "nature abhors a vacuum," which was his way of saying nature won't let the water come out without anything to fill the space left behind.

A more scientific way to explain it is that the air all around us creates pressure. Air is very light, but it isn't completely weightless, and there are literally miles of the stuff above us, pressing down. This air pressure pushes on the Ping-Pong ball and stops any vacuum from being opened up behind it.

So the real reason why "nature abhors a vacuum" is that to open up a vacuum, you have to push back against all that pressure from the air.

🧠 MASTERMIND FACTS

Talk about vacuums, and many people think immediately of vacuum cleaners. They work by making a vacuum (well, a partial vacuum, meaning just a lower pressure of air inside) using a fan to drive air out.

This creates suction as air rushes into the vacuum cleaner's nozzle, pushed by the pressure of all the air outside the machine. Small objects—e.g., dust, crumbs, small toys—get dragged along with the inrushing air. The suction is essentially the same as that which keeps the Ping-Pong ball in place.

Why not try . . .

You can use other things to block the neck of the bottle, too. Try putting a postcard or playing card on top of the bottle, holding it in place (so it doesn't slide off) as you turn the bottle upside down, and then taking your finger away. In some ways, this looks like an even more surprising trick. Our brains might "tell" us that the Ping-Pong ball was wedged into the neck of the bottle like a cork (even though it wasn't), but there seems to be nothing to stop the card from falling down.

Will the same trick work if the bottle is only half filled with water (and therefore half filled with air)? Try experimenting with different volumes of water to find out how much water you need to keep the card in place.

Colorful

FLOATING PICTURES

Here's a way to make drawings that literally spring off the page.

WHAT YOU'LL NEED

→ Water
→ Dry-erase markers (new ones work best)
→ A ceramic plate

WHAT YOU'LL LEARN

Some pictures can float free of what you draw them on.

HOW LONG YOU'LL NEED

20 minutes

HOW TO DO IT

1. Test all the dry-erase markers to make sure they will work for this activity: Draw one dot on a plate using each marker and add some water. Only if the dots float are the pens suitable. Then, ask your child to draw on the plate. It's best to color in the drawing to make it hold together, although line drawings can work, too.

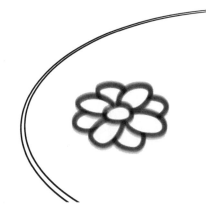

? What happens if you try this with regular felt-tip pens?

Colorful

2. Pour some warm water slowly onto the plate.

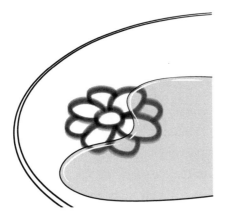

3. The drawing should separate from the surface of the plate and float on top.

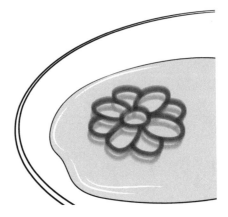

4. Try blowing it around with a straw.

5. Make a whole scene and watch the pieces float around one another!

Why not try . . .

After you have finished playing with the floating drawings, try putting paper on top of the water to transfer the drawings onto it.

WHAT'S GOING ON?

This activity is aimed at promoting creativity more than teaching science. But it works because the ink in the dry-erase markers is a polymer—a kind of plastic—that dries into a solid film and doesn't dissolve in water. It doesn't stick very securely to the smooth ceramic plate (glass works well, too), so water will just lift it off.

MASTERMIND FACTS

Dry-erase markers do pretty much the opposite of normal markers. The ink in permanent markers sticks strongly to almost any surface, so you can't get it off. But the whole point of dry-erase markers is that you can wipe off what you've drawn or written, because it's so weakly stuck to the surface.

But there's a second crucial reason why the drawing gets lifted off by water, which is that the film formed from the dried ink is less dense than water. That's why, as the water slips under the drawing and lifts it free from the surface, the drawing gets carried to the top of the water like a bobbing cork.

MAGIC COLOR JARS

Mix up the secondary colors—then unmix them again!

WHAT YOU'LL NEED

→ Clear baby oil

→ Water

→ Water-based food coloring: red, yellow, and blue

→ Oil-based food coloring: red, yellow, and blue (this type can be sourced online; it is sometimes called "candy color" and is used for coloring chocolate)

→ Three glass jars with lids

WHAT YOU'LL LEARN

Each secondary color (orange, green, and purple) comes from mixing two of the three primary colors (red, yellow, and blue).

HOW LONG YOU'LL NEED

25 minutes

HOW TO DO IT

1. First, half-fill each of the jars with water and mix a few drops of the water-based food coloring into each jar (use one color in each). Stir to mix the color well.

2. Then fill the rest of each jar with baby oil. Because the oil is less dense than the water—this means that an equal amount of the oil weighs less—it will float on top.

? What colors should we mix to get yellow when we are mixing not paint but light?

154

3. Now mix a few drops of one of the oil-based food colorings into the oil layer. Make sure it's not the same color as the water layer—put yellow on top of the blue, red on top of the yellow, and blue on top of the red.

4. Seal the jars with the lids, and ask your child to give them a good shake. You might need to do some shaking yourself, as it has to be quite vigorous to get the oil and water to mix.

5. As the liquids mix, so do the colors. The red and yellow turn orange; the blue and yellow turn green; and the red and blue turn purple.

6. The liquids will separate again quite quickly, and you'll see them return to the two primary colors—perhaps not perfectly, as some of each food coloring may have become dissolved in the other layer. Then you can shake again.

WHAT'S GOING ON?

There are just three primary colors: red, yellow, and blue. You can't get these by mixing any other colors: that's the definition of "primary."

There are three secondary colors, each of them a mixture of two primaries. You probably know already from mixing paints that yellow and blue, say, will mix to make green. We're doing just the same mixing when we shake the jar with yellow and blue oil and water. The oil and water will break up into tiny droplets that, when all jumbled together, will make green, just like the jumbling of the little particles of colored pigment in paint. The difference, though, is that they will slowly separate again because oil and water don't mix. This mixing is what we do when we shake

vinegar (which is watery) and oil to make salad dressing.

MASTERMIND FACTS

Making colors by mixing other colors is what all painters do, and your children will learn how to do it with paints. It's not just the secondary colors that get made this way, but also colors like pink (red and white) and gray (black and white), which don't appear in the rainbow.

TV sets and color screens also make lots of colors by mixing just three primary colors in different amounts. But here things are a little different. If you look very close up at a TV set (don't do it for long, as it's not good for your eyes), you'll see that the three primaries are different: red, blue, and green. If you find a white patch of

Why not try . . .

You can make the color-mixing permanent by adding a few drops of dish soap to your jars before you shake. The dish soap contains soap molecules that will cover the surface of the oil droplets with a water-soluble coat. Some store-bought salad dressings have molecules like this—not soap!—already added to keep them well mixed.

screen, you can see all three of them as tiny colored patches next to one another.

But wait—green?! Why not yellow? And how come these three primary colors make white in these screens, whereas if you mixed paints with those colors, you'd just get a murky brown? The difference is that TV screens mix not food colorings or paints but pure light itself. Mixing light has different rules. In that case, red and green mix to make yellow, while red, green, and blue mix to make white. If the colored patches on the screen are small enough, we can't tell them apart, and the colors mix directly in our eyes.

Mixing paints or dyes or inks is called subtractive mixing, while mixing light is called additive mixing. If it sounds confusing, don't worry—it confused some scientists and artists for many years after the rules of additive mixing were discovered by Sir Isaac Newton in the seventeenth century.

Colorful

PAINTING ON ICE

Here's a way to make pictures that never dry.

WHAT YOU'LL NEED

→ Paints and a paintbrush
→ A slab of ice (freeze water in a dish or flat tray)
→ Tray or large plate to hold the ice

WHAT YOU'LL LEARN

That painting doesn't have to be done on paper!

HOW LONG YOU'LL NEED

20 minutes

The ice needs to be prepared in advance.

HOW TO DO IT

1. Take out the pre-prepared ice from its container and set it top-side down on the tray or large plate, so that you have a smooth surface to paint on.

2. Then simply let the art commence!

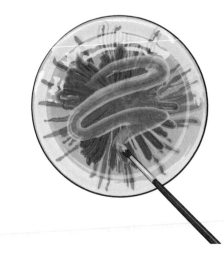

3. With round ice slabs made in a plate or saucer, the ice might be pushed around in a circle by the brush. That's fine—it gives kids a feeling for the slipperiness of ice, and makes the painting motion even more tactile.

Why not try . . .

For variation, you could freeze other objects like glitter or pieces of foil into the ice.

 Have you ever tried dropping oil paint onto water and then floating a piece of paper on top?

 WHAT'S GOING ON?

You can never finish the painting on ice: by the time you finish your masterpiece, the ice melts and washes it away, so you are always in the process of creating something new.

This is a fun opportunity to talk about ice. What is it made from? How come the water has hardened? Why is ice so cold? Why is it slippery? How long will the painting last before it melts—and what happens when it does? Simply ask questions and explore the answers.

MASTERMIND FACTS

So why is the ice hard? All liquids will freeze if they're cold enough, and many solids will melt if they're hot enough. Rocks melt in the hot depths of Earth to make lava, which can escape through volcanic eruptions.

Metals are melted so that they can be cast into shapes: bronze statues, for example. The difference between solids and liquids is that in solids, all the atoms or molecules are packed together and can't move around, whereas in liquids, they can move past one another.

And why is ice slippery? There was a long argument about this in the nineteenth century. Some scientists thought that the surface of the ice melted when it was squeezed, for example, by the pressure of a foot or the blade of an ice skate. Others said that right at the surface the ice was never fully frozen in the first place—there is always a very thin layer of liquid on it—and that's what makes it slippery. We now know that this second idea is right, although squeezing might cause some extra melting, too.

HIDDEN COLORS

When the words get wet, they reveal their true colors.

WHAT YOU'LL NEED

→ Water
→ Colored felt-tip pens (make sure they're not permanent markers)
→ Black permanent marker
→ Paper towel
→ Dropper or pipette

WHAT YOU'LL LEARN

To read and spell colors—in a way they won't forget!

HOW LONG YOU'LL NEED

20 minutes

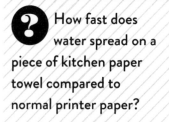 How fast does water spread on a piece of kitchen paper towel compared to normal printer paper?

HOW TO DO IT

1. Here's the effect: the names of the colors (red, blue, etc.) appear in black on the paper towel. But when the child drips water onto each one with the dropper, the corresponding color magically seeps out from each word.

2. Here's how to do it: First, write the name of each color onto the paper towel with the corresponding felt-tip pen.

Colorful

3. Then carefully write over it with the black permanent marker.

4. You're all ready for the trick. Have your child drip water onto the paper using the dropper, and voilà!

5. You could see if the child recognizes the words before testing out to see what color they produce.

 WHAT'S GOING ON?
Permanent markers use ink that sticks firmly to whatever surface it is written on, and their ink doesn't dissolve in water.

Ordinary felt-tip pens, meanwhile, are filled with ink that dissolves in water. So when water soaks into the paper towel, the hidden colored ink gets carried away with it, while the black ink stays stuck to the fibers of the paper towel.

 MASTERMIND FACTS
Why does water soak into the paper, anyway? It's not that the water is "running," exactly. No, it is actually being pulled among the fibers of the paper.

Paper is made of tiny little fibers all crisscrossing and stuck together, with little gaps among them too small to see. The water gets pulled into these gaps by surface tension: a kind of pull created by the water's surface. You can see this surface tension in action in the way water curves upward where it meets the glass walls of a beaker.

Surface tension also allows you to overfill a glass very slightly without it overflowing, if you're careful: it pulls the edge of the surface down to meet the glass rim. When surface tension pulls a liquid through a tangled mat of fibers, it is called wicking. It's what pulls molten wax up a candle wick to burn at the tip.

Why not try . . .

This activity is perfect for teaching the names of colors in different languages.

YOUR OWN PRINTING PRESS!

Make colorful prints using aluminum foil.

WHAT YOU'LL NEED

→ A big roll of aluminum foil

→ Paints and brushes

→ Paper

WHAT YOU'LL LEARN

This is a fun art activity, but it also teaches a simple way of making prints.

HOW LONG YOU'LL NEED

20 minutes

HOW TO DO IT

1. Roll out the foil.

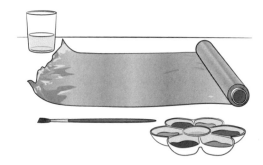

2. Give your child the paints, and off they go!

3. When they have painted their picture, lay a clean piece of paper on top of it and press gently all over. Lift off—and you have a print.

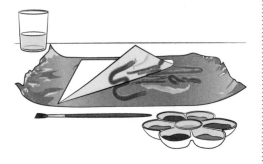

? Why not explore the practice of brass rubbing, where people take a piece of paper, lay it over a brass image, and rub a soft pencil over it to reproduce the image? Can you try making a rubbing of something at home with a crayon?

 WHAT'S GOING ON?

There's no big science behind this activity, but you might like to explore the way that the print is the mirror image of the original painting: a left hand becomes a right hand, and vice versa (try it with paint handprints).

This is also an opportunity to explore the properties of different materials: the foil crinkles more easily than paper, and it holds on to its altered shape if scrunched—it's less springy. It's also not absorbent: the paint doesn't dry quickly like it does on paper, which is why you can make prints this way.

MASTERMIND FACTS

Making prints from metal surfaces is a very old process, dating back at least to the Middle Ages.

Artists would use hard, sharp metal tools to cut their pictures or designs into flat metal plates—usually copper, which is softer than steel. Then they would spread ink over the surface of the plate, maybe using a roller, and place paper on top, gently squeezing it onto the engraved surface in a special press. That's how delicate black-and-white engravings were made, although you could also use colored inks, hand-painted onto the metal plate, to produce color prints. From the late eighteenth century, steel plates were sometimes used: they were more hard-wearing, keeping their sharp edges and fine lines even after many printings—which was good if you were making, say, many copies of an illustrated book, or banknotes.

Why not try . . .

Another way of making prints is to cover leaves, Bubble Wrap, sandpaper, or any textured surface with paint and press it against the paper. See what different textures you can create this way, and maybe use them as part of a painting—say, of a tree or a sandy beach.

TheDadLab

CANDY KALEIDOSCOPE

Make gorgeous rainbow patterns from a package of candy.

WHAT YOU'LL NEED

→ A package of colored candies such as M&M's, Skittles, or Smarties
→ Warm water
→ A large plate

WHAT YOU'LL LEARN

There's cool science here, but it's mostly about seeing an amazing colorful pattern.

HOW LONG YOU'LL NEED

10 minutes

? Have you ever tried dropping a small amount of food coloring into a glass of water? What does it do? Check if the temperature of water changes the process somehow.

HOW TO DO IT

1. Place the candies in a large multicolored circle around the edge of the plate in a pattern.

2. Pour warm water into the center of the plate until the puddle reaches the circle of candies.

3. The color from the candies quickly starts to dissolve in the water—and creates colored streaks that run like rainbow spokes into the center.

Colorful

Try different candies, different shapes, maybe even try making a drawing with the candies, and different color combinations. See how water temperature influences the experiment.

WHAT'S GOING ON?

It's no mystery that the food dyes in brightly colored candies dissolve in water. But why do they form these amazing spoke patterns?

Once again, it's about density. It's not just the dye that dissolves, but also the sugar in the candy coating. And that, as we saw earlier with salt (see page 50), makes the water a bit more dense. So it flows downhill toward the center of the plate, carrying the dye with it.

Some people are surprised that the colors don't mix sideways. But that's a much slower process than the downhill flow. It will happen as the molecules of the dye drift randomly through the water, a process called diffusion. If there aren't any currents in the water to carry the dye with them, it takes some time for the dye to mix well.

MASTERMIND FACTS

Water currents caused by differences in density also occur in the oceans, owing to the amount of dissolved stuff in the water. When water evaporates from the ocean's surface, it leaves the salt behind. So the sea water gets more and more salty, which makes it denser, and it starts to sink to the bottom. The sinking of salty water helps to drive a huge conveyor belt–like circulation of water in the world's oceans. This circulation carries warmer water from the tropics toward the poles, and so it helps to even out differences in heat between the two regions.

A current of warmer water coming from the Gulf of Mexico, called the Gulf Stream, crosses the North Atlantic Ocean and reaches the coast of western Europe, bringing heat with it. If it weren't for this current, northern Europe would have a colder climate.

COLORED SHADOWS

Make shadows brighter with colors.

WHAT YOU'LL NEED

→ Three identical flashlights
→ Sheet of white paper or cardstock
→ Permanent marker pens in green, red, and blue
→ Objects to make shadows, such as a chess piece
→ Clear tape that can be written over

WHAT YOU'LL LEARN

How mixing colored light is different from mixing colored paint.

HOW LONG YOU'LL NEED

20 minutes

HOW TO DO IT

1. Cover the lens of each flashlight with the tape.

? What colors are produced if you use two figurines in front of the screen, where two of their shadows overlap? Can you think why?

169

2. Color the tape on each flashlight with one of the colored markers. (You could mark the flashlights on a side to remind you easily which color it is.)

3. Place the piece of paper upright on the table like a screen, and arrange the flashlights in front, angled so that they will all illuminate the same spot on the paper.

4. In a darkened room, turn the flashlights on. What color does each flashlight make separately on the screen? What color do they all make together?

5. Place objects in front of the screen and look at the shadows they cast. There are three of these—one for each flashlight. What color are they?

WHAT'S GOING ON?

Mixing colored light is not like mixing paints. If you mix red and green light, you get yellow, while blue and green make cyan, and red and blue make magenta.

This seems odd, because red and green paint just make a kind of dirty brown. But it turns out that if red and green light hits our eye, the eye sends the same signal to the brain as it does if yellow light hits the eye.

Stranger still, all three colors mixed together—red, green, and blue light— make white light.

Each of the three shadows produced by the object appear where the figurine blocks out the light from one of the flashlights, so that only that of the other two flashlights can be seen. So the three shadows have the colors of these three blends of colored light: red/green (yellow), green/blue (cyan), and blue/red (magenta).

MASTERMIND FACTS

Sunlight is "white light": it makes a piece of white paper look that color, whereas if you shine colored light on the paper, it will seem to take on the same hue. But this white sunlight has a whole rainbow of colors "hidden" within it. While you see in this experiment that you can make white light from mixing blue, red, and green light, the white light of sunlight is a mix of many colors: yellow, orange, red, green, blue, and purple/violet.

You can separate out these colors using a glass prism. As the light passes through it, the rays get spread out into bands of each different color, called the

Why not try . . .

Your child might like to stage a play in front of the paper using toys, with the flashlights as stage lighting. Let her or him experiment with moving the flashlights to get different lighting effects and color mixtures.

spectrum. The same thing happens when sunlight passes through a glass of water. The spectrum is created because the light rays bend as they pass into and out of the prism or the water, but rays of each different color are bent by different amounts.

Rainbows are formed by raindrops acting like little prisms. The sun's rays enter the water droplet and get reflected from the inside surface, as if from a mirror—but they also get bent so that the different colors are spread out. To see a rainbow, the sun has to be behind us and the raindrops in the sky in front of us. The light rays pass overhead into the droplets, which reflect them back to our eyes, spread out into a spectrum.

Afterword

I hope you have liked this book; I had a lot of fun writing it and even learned some new things. I encourage you to continue doing projects with your children after finishing this book. If you want to get more ideas, you can find them on my website, www .thedadlab.com, where I post new experiments, tips, reviews of kids' toys and books, and more.

As I hope you can see, the emphasis of *TheDadLab* is on the family: on spending time together. Your children will learn something along the way for sure, but the most important thing to have learned is not some scientific facts but the idea that curiosity and creativity are important and that the best way to learn is to be open, to explore, to ask questions, to try things out and see what happens—and to have fun while doing it together!

This openness and exploration are vital.

These experiments are not prescriptions but suggestions—make sure you listen to your children and adapt projects to their needs and interests. What you think is the most important aspect of an experiment is not necessarily what will captivate them the most, so go where their curiosity leads.

The aim is to grow a generation of creative and curious people—because the world needs them. We can do that together.

@TheDadLab

https://www.instagram.com/thedadlab/

https://www.facebook.com/thedadlab/

https://www.facebook.com/groups/ TheDadLab/

https://www.youtube.com/c/thedadlab

https://twitter.com/thedadlab

Acknowledgments

There is a long list of people who helped to make this book possible, and I am grateful to them all.

First, I would like to thank my family. To my curious sons, Alex and Max, for constantly challenging me with questions I do not know the answers to, for inspiring me every day. To my better half, Tania, for sharing TheDadLab journey with me, for being my trusted adviser, and for supporting me every step of the way.

A very special thank-you to my literary agent, Kathleen Ortiz, for successfully convincing me that a regular person like me can write a book and for taking my hand and guiding me through it all.

My abundant thanks to my editor, Lauren Appleton, whose passion and insight had a huge impact on this book. Thank you, too, to Marian Lizzi and Rachel Ayotte, who took over when Lauren was on maternity leave, for their passion for TheDadLab and belief in me.

I am grateful to Philip Ball, for going in-depth on the science behind our projects with me and for his wise counsel.

Thanks, too, to Olga Trifonova for creating wonderful step-by-step illustrations for this book. Without them, this book wouldn't be the same.

A big thank-you to Pauline Neuwirth for designing this book and making it look amazing.

And finally, but most important, to my community. To you, TheDadLab readers and online fans, for your support and for allowing me to be that extra link connecting you and your children.

Index

Index

Index